The
Secret Language
of
Girlfriends

. . . .

Karen Neuburger

WITH NADINE SCHIFF

NEW YORK

The Secret Language of Girlfriends

of

**TALKING LOUDLY, LAUGHING WILDLY,
AND MAKING THE MOST OF OUR MOST IMPORTANT
FRIENDSHIPS**

HYPERION

Library of Congress Cataloging-in-Publication Data

Neuburger, Karen.
   The secret language of girlfriends : talking loudly, laughing wildly, and making the
most of our most important friendships / by Karen Neuburger with Nadine Schiff.
      p. cm.
   ISBN 1-4013-0163-0
   1. Female friendship. 2. Interpersonal relations. 3. Women—Psychology. I. Schiff,
Nadine. II. Title

BF575.F66N485 2005
158.2'5'082—dc22   2004059771

Hyperion books are available for special promotions and premiums. For details
contact Michael Rentas, Assistant Director, Inventory Operations, Hyperion, 77 West
66th Street, 11th floor, New York, New York 10023, or call 212-456-0133.

Designed by Lorelle Graffeo

FIRST EDITION

10   9   8   7   6   5   4   3   2   1

To Oprah:

*My angel in PJs—may you always be comfortable.
You always see the grandness in ordinary people,
thank you for seeing it in me.*

Contents

Acknowledgments

From Karen

OVER THE LAST ten years I've crisscrossed the country and had a ball at more than three hundred pajama parties, meeting thousands of amazing women along the way. I had a dream to record the stories of friendship and sisterhood these women have told me, and my dream has come to life with this book. So to all the women who have shared their funny, tender, and intimate secrets with me as only women can, I want to say thank you in the most warm, sincere way. You have truly taught me the Secret Language of Girlfriends.

Thank you to Nadine Schiff, my cowriter, who helped me convey my memories with smart and witty bravado, retold my stories with heartfelt sentiment and inspiration, and sifted through hundreds of letters to uncover the Secret Language within. I couldn't have done this without you.

To the wonderful women in my personal Broad Squad, who were the "research lab" for this book as well as its inspiration:

Cathie, Mary, Vickie, Tina, and that true girl's girl, Jillian Manus. To all my girlfriends at Hyperion, who not only lived and breathed the Secret Language of Girlfriends for this book, but personally practice it: Kelly Notaras, our editor, a genius with words and wisdom—and a blast at a PJ party; Jane Comins, Katie Wainwright, and Karin Maake for their tireless efforts to get the word out; and especially to Ellen Archer, for seeing the girlfriend movement, and Bob Miller, for letting the girls run with the project.

To the team at Karen Neuburger, thank you for your time, support, and talent. From the tedious copying to creative design, this was a team effort.

To Richard, my husband, a big thank-you for letting me be brutally honest and for your great sense of humor. Humor brought us together and keeps us together. Thank you for understanding my need for girl time, and for your never-ending support.

Finally, thank you to my two best girlfriends: my daughters, AJ and Dany. Dany was my lifeline from one lifetime to another, and she has kept me grounded, determined, and independent ever since. Dany, you continue to make me proud of you and to inspire me with the family values that influence every decision you make. You are more fun than you know. Thank you to AJ, my midlife daughter whose birth prompted me to live my life for comfort. As demanding of herself as she is of her relationships, compromise has not yet entered her vocabulary. Thank you, AJ, for keeping me young, cool, and dancing.

From Nadine

TO KAREN—for sharing her soul with a stranger.

TO JILLIAN AND CATHIE—for putting us together and making us friends.

TO ALL THE FOLKS AT HYPERION—especially Kelly and Ellen—who understand the importance of talking loudly and laughing wildly.

TO ELLEN, MAIA, AND DRU for their expert assistance.

TO MY MOTHER, DENA.

TO MY BROAD SQUAD—Annie, Barbara, Cristina, Genevieve, Jan, Maria, Nancy, Pamela, Ruth, Susan D., Sarah H., Susan H., Wanda, and my most special addition: Sara Rosen. And to all the girls in my life, big and little, who don't just talk the talk...but walk me through every day.

YOUR SECRETS ARE SAFE WITH ME.

Chapter One

The Broad Squad

Broad Squad \ 'bröd 'skwäd\ A group of girlfriends who totally have your back . . . but always put you out in front.

JUST AS WOMEN need more than one color of lipstick and nail polish in our beauty arsenal, so too do we all need our Broad Squad to get us through the insanity of our lives. As modern divas, we exist in crisis mode most of the time. When you consider the tribulations of marriage, children, divorce, remarriage, promotions, and firings, it's amazing we all aren't melting down daily. (Which of course we are, which is why we need to carry a cell phone at all times to call one another.) Add to the drama-queen list the traumas of Botox, men, reunions, men, not to mention short skirts being back in style, and it's not exactly news we all need a team of girl-friends to survive life in the "pink zone."

Your Broad Squad should be a highly trained special unit—heat-seeking missiles specializing in pleasure seeking and covert male surveillance. As your allies and accomplices for life, they should always make you feel cherished and pampered, like the babe magnet you were born to be. The truth is, if real life hadn't gotten in the way, your Broad Squad could spend years together, yakking it up about everything from politics to religion, career aspirations to hair length. A good Broad Squad possesses a variety of skills, including but not limited to how to wreak revenge on an evil boss, how to sniff out if your man is cheating, and how to free you from a boring dinner party in less than ten minutes.

Even though we all speak the secret language of girlfriends, at times we require a particular dialect. Hormonal mood changes (from that time of month to the dreaded change) have their own languages, distinct from, for example, the language of bathing suit season (and its requisite exposure of our dimpling thighs). Thus we need an array of girlfriends with diverse talents always at the ready.

Let me clarify. Having a full-on Broad Squad isn't like needing a fifth for mahjong. We're talking crucial here, a trained attack team, a girlfriend posse to ride shotgun and make sure your back (and every other part of your anatomy) is well covered.

If you have very good karma, you may be lucky enough to have one girlfriend who has every great quality you could ever possibly desire. She can handle any situation on her own. Lucky you! But others of us have different specialists on call for each situation. Whether you have five girlfriends or one, here are the bottom-line needs of every girlfriend's Broad Squad.

❧ The Old Friend ☙

Old Friend \'ōld 'frend\ The girlfriend who convinced us we looked beautiful on prom night even when we wore braces and stuffed athletic socks in our bras for enhanced cleavage.

There's a song: "Make new friends, but keep the old; one is silver and the other's gold." Every Broad Squad needs that one friend who goes for the gold. She's the one we bonded with in pajamas while drooling over glossy photos of some teen idol on a Saturday-night sleepover. We yapped on the telephone three times a day about absolutely nothing, although we were sure we were in the middle of some life-altering drama. Our oldest friend is a walking memory book, the one who reminds us of the embarrassing nicknames and outrageous hairstyles of our past. She is our hope chest, the girlfriend who thinks of us as her good china and crystal glasses. Unconditionally caring, she believes in our C-rating (that is to say, our cuteness factor) even as our body parts surrender to gravity.

Vickie is my oldest friend, my protector and guardian since the third grade. Together, we blazed a ridiculous style trail from Girl Scout uniforms to poodle skirts to cowboy vests and tie-dyed T-shirts, without ever reporting each other to the fashion police.

CONFIDENTIALLY YOURS . . .

To ease one friend's aching heart on a night too cold to go out on the town, a group of college girlfriends threw an Estrogen Party. Decked in their comfiest pajamas and frizziest bed heads, the girls were greeted at the door by a sign reading OVARIES ONLY. They concocted and drank girlie cocktails—Cosmos and Georgia Peaches—and listened to a specially selected playlist of exclusively female pop stars. The dangerous combination of catchy pop music and vodka prompted some girls to bust out their karaoke skills. Martinis in hand, the girls danced the night away to Janet, Christina, and Madonna, and even capped it all off with a snowball fight. The guest of honor forgot all about her less-than-worthy ex and remembered what a blast it is to hang exclusively with the girls.

Well, except that one time. As a flat-chested, no-hips teenager I was desperate to transform myself into a Marilyn Monroe pinup. With no push-up bras or falsies to expand on what Mother Nature had clearly forgotten, I took the do-it-yourself route. I stuffed every pair of athletic socks I owned into my bra and panties, hoping to fill out my chest, hips, and tush. My new headlights positioned under a royal blue angora sweater, I thought I was one hot mama. That is, until Vickie informed me that the other kids were writing in her yearbook that I looked like a walking sock puppet. Mortified, I tossed my socks back in my drawer—and I became as God intended for me to be.

At school, Vickie and I majored in each other, faithfully recording each other's periods in our school binders. Clueless as we were, nothing could stop us from endlessly lecturing each other about driving too fast, drinking too much, and messing with boys. More than once we tested our tolerance for alcohol on sloe gin, escaped together out my bedroom window, and noiselessly pushed the family car down the alley to take midnight cruises.

It's been forty years since Vickie and I, underaged and overzealous, tried to talk our way into the bars in northern Wisconsin so we could drink beer and dance. She was always the angel on my shoulder, warning me to slow down as we cruised the streets in my family's fabulous green 409 Pontiac. Driving with the top down even in the ten-degree-below midwestern winter, we blared Roy Orbison's "Cryyyyying Over You." Vickie and I cried too . . . from freezing our rear ends off.

But the biggest crisis was yet to come. Nineteen years old and a sophomore in college, I received what seemed like the worst possible news: a pregnancy test came out positive. Discovering you're about to be an unwed mother in a small midwestern town is bad enough; try finding out your boyfriend, the charismatic quarterback, has another girl in the family way at the very same time. Talk about redefining the term *touchdown*.

Who was there to see me through my shame? Who took on the unpaid job of being my bodyguard, accompanying me on frequent bathroom runs and intimidating anyone who dared wonder out loud why I fell asleep at my desk or why I never took off my coat in class anymore? My savior, my soulmate, my oldest friend: Vickie.

✎ *The Best Friend* ✎

Best Friend \\'best 'frend\ The one you confide all your secrets to . . . including your on-line dating disasters, real bra size, and the exact number of unpaid parking tickets in your glove compartment.

BEST FRIENDS AND DAUGHTERS

Now that my daughters are getting older, they're moving up the charts into the "best friend" slot as well. (Yes, it's possible to have three best friends.) Dany, now with her own family, bosses me around and keeps me totally grounded. My eighteen-year-old, AJ, is a free spirit who dances to the tune of her own drummer. These best friends both love grilling me about my younger days and plying me for my most embarrassing moments . . . which unfortunately exist in abundance.

Besides the belly laughs and the secret language we share, together we can eat a giant tuna casserole or a huge bowl of shrimp dip in one sitting. If I have taught them anything, it's that good food and best friends always have a way of showing up at the party together.

It's-Not-a-Party-Without-It Shrimp Dip

(Aunt Vrony's Dip)

2 8-ounce packages cream cheese (full strength, not light)

¼ cup milk (1% is fine)

2 tablespoons Miracle Whip salad dressing (not mayo!)

1 cup Parmesan cheese

2 teaspoons crushed garlic

2 4-ounce cans deveined shrimp

¼ teaspoon paprika

sprig parsley

Put cream cheese, milk, and Miracle Whip in a mixing bowl. Mix with electric beater on medium until soft, creamy, and totally blended. (Use fingers to taste.) Add in the Parmesan cheese and crushed garlic; blend. Drain shrimp, keeping a little of the juice for flavor. Fold shrimp and juice into mixture. Taste again liberally, then garnish with paprika and parsley. Chill for about 1 hour.

Serve with Triscuits, or your favorite dipping crackers, chips, or veggies.

Every girl needs a friend known as the vault, the broad in your squad who would submit to persecution before ever sharing the intimate details of your sordid life. My best friend Mary has been the keeper of my secrets for thirty years. In good times, our secret language allows us to finish each other's sentences; in bad times we require no conversation at all. Just when I've hit rock bottom, she shows up to drag me out to a karaoke bar or to show me how to get rid of the orange tint from one of my all-too-frequent self-tanning disasters.

This woman moves with the speed of a freight train to make sure everything in my life is in operational order. Each year we watch the Miss America pageant together, and every time we have a heated three-hour debate (over red wine and Ho-Hos) as to why looking great in a bikini qualifies you for a scholarship.

Mary has been there for me during crisis times as well. Thirty years ago when I got divorced, as I sat paralyzed on a recycled Piggly Wiggly box, she single-handedly packed up my home and moved me and my daughter Dany into a new town house—all in under twelve hours. Let's just say, marital circumstances being what they were (and they weren't good), Mary forced me to leave behind my silver-edged Rosenthal china and Bavarian crystal and focus on the essentials: stuffed animals, a stereo, and one cozy worn sofa. As I sat comatose on that sofa, eating powdered-sugar doughnuts, Mary and my daughter unpacked, turned on the stereo, and sang show tunes all night long.

She is still the only person I know I can call at three A.M. and have it be okay, the only person who always makes the cut on my guest list. Whether we're engaging in retail therapy, sipping daiquiris on a cruise, or inhaling macaroni and cheese in my kitchen, Mary's the one I want to share everything with.

DEAR KAREN

Dear Karen,

My best friend and college roommate Mel and I have been friends for 23 years. When we need a fix, we call each other with our special language code phrase, which is "I need a Heidi" or "I need a Melanie." We both know exactly what that means. It means we have to see each other in an emergency 911 way.

Heidi
Brewster, New York

The Concierge

Concierge \'kän-sē-'erzh\ The girlfriend who knows the best restaurants with the cutest waiters and has the phone numbers for both.

We all need a girlfriend in our posse who treats us as if we live in a suite at the Four Seasons and who understands our life was meant to be filled with fluffy towels and mints on our pillows. She makes the best hostess in the group, and she's the one you defer to when nobody can decide where to go to dinner. If your Broad Squad is heading off on a trip together, she's the one who'll actually remember to bring the map.

Tina is my friend who knows everything truly important in life: how to get wine stains out of lingerie (no questions asked), how to find the cheapest airfares, and whether to wear silver or gold shoes with a champagne suit (I'm never sure!). When I'm having a really bad hair day, Tina slips me the latest concoction her star hairdresser whipped up, even though it's not officially on the market. She is my greatest advocate, my personal encyclopedia, and my designated driver. She can walk into any party and immediately identify the players by their drinks (whether it's a Jack Daniel's or a martini/Cosmo crowd). Tina is an invaluable member of my Broad Squad, and I wouldn't even try to get through life without her.

⸱ The Personal Coach ⸱

Personal Coach \ˈpər-sə-nəl ˈkōch\ Our one-woman cheer-leading squad; she never attempts to look better in a short skirt and pom-poms than we do.

She is our positive-attitude, glass-half-full friend, who may drive us crazy with her cheery optimism but will never let us underestimate or shortchange ourselves. Each time we're convinced Prince Charming has finally arrived on a white horse to rescue us from our day job, she's the one who grills him on his intentions—just to make sure he's good enough. She cheers us on to that promotion, thrilled our success is tax deductible. She raves about our achievements to everyone, inspiring us to dream the impossible dream . . . while remaining fully awake and solvent.

My friend Jillian is my cheerleader. A larger-than-life woman, she is a classic diva who moonlights as my full-time personal support system. Feathering my face with a perfect pink blush and pushing me into territory I've never been before, she constantly challenges me. In her eyes, I am always the queen, capable of doing whatever it takes if I just put my mind to it. Her optimism is not only infectious but inspiring. Even when Jillian is not physically with me, her can-do voice pops up in my head in moments of crisis. In her high heels and classic suit, she strides ahead, leaving negativity in her wake.

The "Just Say Yes" Girlfriend

"Just Say Yes" Girlfriend \'jəst 'sā 'yes 'gər(-ə)l-'frənd\ The girlfriend on your team who celebrates the essence of you every day, making you feel like the guest of honor at your own party. Accessories: glittery shoes, henna tattoos, and one hot concert ticket.

This is the broad in our squad who is our "just say yes" girl, even when all around us people seem to be saying no. She's the one who gets us revved up about sewing new slipcovers for the couch, even though we failed home ec and barely notice the melted Raisinet stains anymore. When we're determined to be depressed, she shows up at our door, ordering us to ditch our big bag of M&M's (and our bathrobe) for a night of embarrassing karaoke. Her enthusiasm for us is so unconditionally infectious, we could tell her our most depraved secrets and her response would be to love us even more.

I think of my friend Donna as the social director of my Broad Squad. She is the one who convinces me to leave my work and family behind and join her screaming in the front row for Elton John or the Rolling Stones. Always insisting I wiggle into last year's jeans, she paints my face with lots of goop and sets my eyes with three layers of thick black mascara. Before I know it, I am dancing in the aisles, arms flung heavenward, underarm flab be damned.

Donna really does make me feel that I am celebrated every day. Not only is she a great listener, she is the queen of the sample sales, always finding me glittery tops and satin shoes that make me feel like writing up a guest list and menu for a party I want to throw. Every Broad Squad needs one member who gets your mojo up and running and keeps you in a party frame of mind.

Broad Squad Additions

If you think of your Broad Squad as the main food group, now you have all your essential nutrients and can add on with specialty items. There are stages in our lives when we meet new people, as a result of dealing with crazy-making situations such as becoming a bride, becoming a new mother, or enrolling at a mature age at community college. We all like bonding with other

SECRET LANGUAGE GLOSSARY

The great part about sharing a secret language is that it takes only a few words to convey a huge idea. Here are some of the phrases we use in our girl-friend lexicon.

I'm Upset

CODE FOR: The world is now all about me. Do not talk about you. In fact, don't even mention you. At this minute I have no patience for rational thought. Simply agree with me and tell me you'd feel the same, even though your gut tells you I'm probably suffering from temporary insanity.

I Need to Talk

CODE FOR: Drop everything and come over immediately. Pretend that you have all day to listen to me, even though you know I'll blow it out in under an hour. If you cannot see

(cont.)

me in person and must speak over the telephone (a totally second best choice), make sure I cannot hear you opening your e-mail or washing dishes while I'm catharting.

I Don't Have Anything to Wear

CODE FOR: I'm stressed, fat, old, and ugly and cannot abide standing under fluorescent lights to try anything on. What I want is for you to lend me a perfect outfit with matching shoes. Girlfriend code dictates an open-closet policy.

Do I Have Food in My Teeth?

CODE FOR: You are so close to me, you can actually tell me the truth about that little piece of spinach caught in the gap between my front teeth. This code also applies to your honest opinion about bad hair

women who are as fanatical as we are so we don't feel so alone. Here are some of those times.

The Mommy Track

Mommy Track \'mä-mē 'trak\ The ability to multitask in a three-ring circus with you as the leader, minus the whip. Must have an ability to conference-call from home while making chocolate chip cookies and racing Hot Wheels.

One of the crazy stages of life, when we all need special reinforcement, has to be motherhood. Having raised two babies to adulthood, I know there are some fun times. But I can distinctly recall a time when my 24/7 companions spent considerable amounts of time drooling, burping, and speaking in monosyllables. In that dirty-diaper phase, what I needed was an adult to talk to. That's why, when you go through this stage, you need someone on your Broad Squad who knows what you're going through. Someone who can obsess with you about baby food (fresh or canned?),

(cont.)

days, bad boyfriends, and wearing anything luminescent like hot pink. The colors may be in style, but you have permission to tell me I look like a psychedelic ice cream cone gone wrong.

Don't Tell a Soul
CODE FOR: Includes your husband or boyfriend. No exceptions!

preschools (which are the best?), fathers (sperm bank or biological?). You need other mothers who've traded in their Gucci bags for diaper bags, who will sit on the park bench next to you as you feed string cheese and carrot sticks into the mouths of your young. It's this companionship alone that will keep you out of this year's most fashionable straitjacket.

PROOF OF THE OBVIOUS

Researchers studying the value of mothering in groups found that female baboons living in the wild in Kenya who formed relationships with other females were more successful at child rearing than those who were isolated. I had to laugh. As if any new mother housebound with a case of cabin fever during a northeastern winter couldn't have told you how easily you can lose your mind alone all day with a crying baby. Hello?

The Cleveland Mamas

I met a group of girls from Cleveland, Ohio, who loved being girlfriends so much during high school, they took their relationship to a whole new adult level. Recently, all four girlfriends were pregnant at the same time (talk about family planning) and had babies within weeks of each other. Real life sometimes is stranger than fiction!

Jennifer, Jenee, Kristen, and Amie met each other years ago at their all-girl high school, where they shared typical teen pastimes like crushes on boys, dancing at mixers, and even a little underaged imbibing. Horrified at the thought of growing up and growing apart, they simply decided to grow up together. Within two years, they had all married, and all took turns wearing (surprisingly tasteful) bridesmaid dresses.

With that first mission accomplished and with a little assist from their husbands, within months all four were pregnant. They enjoyed scintillating discussions of breastfeeding, cracked nipples, baby weight, even morning sickness. They went on doctor visits together, bought maternity clothes en masse, and within months of each other, gave birth to four baby boys.

Jennifer explained to me how great it was to have such a tremendous support network of women. "I could call any one of my friends and get a pep talk whenever I needed it. Husbands don't understand the whole postpartum thing"—you think?—"and so it's a tremendous relief to be able to pick up the phone and have one of your best friends going through the same thing. I consider us to be one another's family. We know from the tone in each other's voices when one of us is headed out the door for a good cry in the car. To have the four of us together so long, still living in the same town, our parents here—I feel so fortunate. We are quite the all-girl squad."

❦ The New Friend ❧

New Friend \'nü 'frend\ The one you meet through school or work who has your Broad Squad up in jealous arms. Introduce her slowly and carefully to the other women on your team so they can see how much she has to offer. Accessories: a great smile and a warning to your Broad Squad to tread gently.

So maybe you're not having a baby, not going back to school, not joining the local canasta club. Maybe your Broad Squad already feels complete. But there's always room for one more at the martini bar. One day some great lady is bound to show up on your radar unexpectedly. You'll spend all night talking and wonder if you were twins separated at birth. As we get older (and let's face it, we can't pretend it's not happening), a magnificent thing happens: We are drawn to other women who have similar interests and time schedules.

A couple of years ago, I decided that between my family, my business, my travel schedule, and my cottage garden, I

CONFIDENTIALLY YOURS . . .

A friend of mine who moved from one coast to the other let me in on a little secret. She said that even though she was sad to leave her good friends behind, she looked forward to meeting and making new friends because this time she could do it on her own terms. Now she could make friends not because of her husband's business or her children's schools, but because she genuinely wanted to spend time with new girlfriends. A good lesson for us all at any stage of our lives.

---

wasn't giving myself time to connect to other women. So for the first time in a long time, I started making and accepting luncheon invites and joining some women's organizations. Not only did I make some really fabulous new friends, but they introduced me to other women who were equally inspiring. And so I formed a kind of second-tier Broad Squad, women who could enhance and add to the beloved team of girlfriends I already had in place.

Ex-Friends

Ex-Friend \'eks-'frend\ The girl in your life who manages to make everything in your life all about her. A traitor who trades your intimate secrets as collateral in the open social market. Accessories: a Dumpster.

One of the harsh realities of girlfriendship is that not all friends are soulmates destined to be part of your life forever. Sometimes a relationship runs its course and you and your friend go your separate ways. This "divorce" happens more often than you may think, and it can be more painful than any breakup with a guy. Sometimes there is a specific inciting incident (for example, she forgot your birthday or went out with your ex), but more often than not, the breakup happens slowly, over time.

Life brings tidal shifts, and not even the best of girlfriends can always swim in the same direction. We may think it's encoded in our DNA to share Reese's Peanut Butter Cups and gossip until death do us part, but sadly, that's not always the case. Marriage, divorce, children, or changing values can come between even the best of friends.

When I was in my twenties, my best friend was also my associate at work. We had so much in common: similar jobs, daughters the same age, tough marriages. We could have been each other's sounding boards and confidantes, helping each other through tough times, but it didn't work out that way. I felt like she made everything between us a competition, making me feel less-than. She constantly pointed out when people sent her bigger bouquets, more gifts, and more business. Her wardrobe was trendier, her daughter smarter, her social life way busier than mine. After a while, I examined our friendship and decided she was a detriment to my confidence and well-being. Looking back now, I realize she was just insecure, and I allowed her to tear me down in order to build herself up. That was my first—and I hope last—experience of a toxic girlfriend relationship.

Lots of people want to ride with you in the limo, but what you want is someone who will take the bus with you when the limo breaks down.

—OPRAH WINFREY

Guys are always amazed by how complicated gal-pal friendships are. But we share so many intimacies, secrets, and vulnerabilities with one other, our relationships often feel far more passionate and emotional than romantic love. (Minus the freak-outs over cellulite and bad hair days.) As I've said, even though every once in a while one of our Broad Squad members may break the girlfriend law (translation: a deep betrayal by a friend, punishable by not taking any of her calls ever again), most of our connections will last through the confusion and strain of everyday life transitions. We all have such a rich history together—better to talk through our differences and move on to the next stage of growing up with our Broad Squad intact. Let's face it: There's always another guy out there somewhere. (At least that's what they say.) But when the chips are down, only your girlfriend knows your favorite flower, your secret shoe store, and your habit of sleeping in your favorite worn-out and faded flannel PJs from high school. Those are the things that matter most!

Chapter Two
Girlfriends and Wellness

Girlfriend-Wellness Connection \'gər(-ə)l-,frend- 'wel-nəs kə-'nək-shən\ The way girlfriends see you through kids, marriage, divorce, illness, and attempted murder caused by hot flashes. Flying across the country, they come to hold your hand or show up at your home at three in the morning with coffee and real cream. When you're as low as you can be, your Broad Squad becomes your estrogen battery. Just plug in and live off the pure girlfriend energy coming to a Girls' Night Out (or In) near you.

ℐF WELLNESS CAN be defined as the balance of mind, body, and spirit, then my girlfriends are the scales that keep me in check. My Broad Squad is hardwired to save my sanity. They listen to my kvetching and therapeutically reassure me they know just what I mean (even when they have no clue what I'm talking about). This lifts the veil off my temporary psychosis every time. As far as my physical body is concerned, when the chips are down—by which I mean that my weight is up, and my thighs are dimpling—I know I can turn to my girlfriends for motivation and support. My Broad Squad is always game for whatever new exercise regime that I swear will prove to be (just like the Prince Charming theory) the one. And when I'm low on spiritual oms and yearn for a solid session of retail therapy (or whatever superficial endeavor I can think of that day), it's my girlfriends who reflect back to me what I cannot see in the mirror of a Barney's dressing room: myself, loved unconditionally.

Having dealt with the issue of wellness for many a moon (and being very involved in the fight against breast cancer), I admit I'm a sucker for new vitamins and minerals. Promise me that you have the magic bullet to renew my tired liver or boost my sluggish metabolism, and I'll follow you anywhere. (Even to the bank, where you're stockpiling my hard-earned cash.) But even though I'll plunk my credit card down for a natural elixir guaranteed to lift my mood, I don't like being held captive by all the sensible rules for staying healthy. Eating a lettuce sandwich while visualizing my glass half full leaves me feeling grumpy, hungry, and emotionally empty. So I have looked into some studies that support my personal beliefs and have come up with my very own formula for staying well.

Karen's Guide to Girlfriends' Good Health

🕴 **FOR A LONG LIFE, EAT LOTS OF CANDY.** That's right. There's something about sweets. They mellow me out and give me a little zing at the same time. All you have to do is take one bite, and you instantly feel a little closer to nirvana.

🕴 **LAUGH!** Take a Girls' Night Out where the focus is on getting a belly laugh. So rent a funny video, watch your favorite sitcom, or buy season tickets to your local comedy club. (Alternatively, you can just hide behind the door and watch your husband try to take care of the kids for an hour. That's a comedy routine all by itself.)

🏃 **Jᴏɪɴ ᴀ ɢɪʀʟ ʙᴀɴᴅ.** It's never too late to become Melissa Etheridge or Sheryl Crow. It's said that women who play a musical instrument stay healthier longer, because they get out of their own minds when they groove to the music. Music soothes the soul . . . and gives you a performance high. Besides, the world needs more girl bands.

🏃 **Tʜɪɴᴋ ɴᴇɢᴀᴛɪᴠᴇʟʏ.** Yes, you heard me! Forget all this positive stuff. As crazy as it sounds, people who are pessimistic and expect everything to go wrong have less anxiety because their expectations are low. So follow your mother's lead and start worrying! Don't look for happiness. Apparently, it will only make you miserable.

🏃 **Cᴇʟᴇʙʀᴀᴛᴇ ʏᴏᴜʀ ᴡʀɪɴᴋʟᴇs.** What's the deal with Botox—freezing your face so you can't smile or cry? Just load up the cake with those candles, girl! If you feel good about getting older, you supposedly live seven and a half years longer than if you're always trying to beat the clock.

🏃 **GET DANCING.** The best cure for the blues and the blahs is to shake your bootie and take a pass around the dance floor. Women who strut their stuff are thought to be healthier than the wallflower who doesn't get her groove on.

🏃 **PURSUE YOUR PASSION.** If you're going to spend two-thirds of your life working, you might as well be having a good time while you're doing it. Passion is an important element in staying alive! Find out what you love to do . . . and then just *do* it.

Running for Wellness

Three Bozeman, Montana, working mothers—Elaine, Sophie, and Olivia—use running as a way to meet, catch up, and keep each other well. So intense is their desire to run together that they leave the warmth of their homes at eight o'clock on Saturday mornings in ten-degree weather. They met while running solo and decided to team up to keep one another inspired.

At first they were cautious with one another, even shy. But as they found their way across well-worn terrain and unexplored territory together, they started to let their guard down. They began to reveal the paths each of their lives had taken, from the roads less traveled to the familiar ones they all shared. Now, the women chat nonstop from one mile to the next. No subject is off-limits, no problem too great; no feelings are left unexplored. No one is afraid of saying the wrong thing.

Collectively they have twelve children! Each one has discovered a lump or lumps in her breast. Thankfully none of these lumps were cancerous, but waiting for the biopsy results was terrifying just the same. As a Jew, a Methodist, and a Catholic, respectively, they have great faith in common. Now they even have hilarious stories of family gatherings, many of which they now all attend. They have mourned the death of a mother from suicide and a father from complications from alcoholism and smoking. And they have feted each other's events: milestone birthdays, children's dance recitals, and exciting job promotions.

They've completed 5Ks, 10Ks, and a marathon, clearing their minds and strengthening their bodies at the same time. They've learned the art of running with a Zen attitude—not competitively, but for and against themselves, appreciating and sustaining their good health. They say that running together has soothed their souls, giving them confidence that their friends are there for them every step of the way.

You've Got to Have Friends

Sometimes it takes a crisis to teach you that friends are the best medication. After an unexpected accident involving her spinal cord, Melanie returned to her empty house alone and scared. A single mother who'd put all of her energy into her teenage daughter, she had no husband or lover to care for her. Her focus had been on raising her child, not creating a support network for herself. Now she was scheduled for major surgery and would need help.

Completely panicked, she quickly began to call friends.

CONFIDENTIALLY YOURS . . .

Medical researchers found that those with friends are more likely to survive a heart attack or major surgery, and less likely to get respiratory infections or cancer. According to a "tend and befriend" study developed by Dr. Shelley E. Taylor at UCLA, women consistently outlive men. Study after study has found that special ties reduce our risk of disease by lowering blood pressure, heart rate, and cholesterol. "There's no doubt," says Dr. Taylor, "that friends are helping us live longer."

On the phone she was calm in describing her nightmarish situation, not wanting to dump her problems on her friends. But invariably that friend would jump in and offer to help in any way she could. Melanie was so taken aback that she would hang up, burst into tears, and sob uncontrollably. It wasn't just the reassurance her friends gave her, it was their willingness to interrupt their own lives to do whatever was necessary for her.

Her friends concocted an elaborate schedule. Veronica kept her company during the long hours of waiting for surgery, and appeared again hours later in the recovery room. Lois flew across the country to assist Melanie during the first week after surgery, helping her get to the bathroom in the middle of the night. Marianna came the second week, as Melanie gained the strength and confidence to shower on her own. Betsy insisted on moving in for the third week, not because Melanie needed help, but because Betsy wanted to keep her company.

Other friends drove her on errands, bought groceries, and took her out to lunch or a movie. What Melanie began to understand was how isolated she had previously been. To enjoy the comfort of friendship, all she had to do was ask. The illness also helped her weed out her friends. Some friends called but barely asked how she was before launching into their own dramas. And there were a few who didn't call at all. She learned who the real members of her Broad Squad were.

What Melanie realized was that she wasn't alone, even

though she lived alone. It had never occurred to her that while she didn't live in a traditional family, she was part of an informal one. The support she received sped her recovery and deepened her healing. And now she was ready to be a friend and accept others into her heart.

Rebecca and Hillary

When Hillary and Rebecca met at their first United Synagogue Youth convention, the then-fourteen-year-old high school freshmen really bonded. Because Hillary lived in Austin and Rebecca in Dallas, they didn't get to see each other often but wrote letters, talked on the phone, and became each other's number one Broad Squad member. They attended all five conventions every year, and Rebecca even visited Hillary in Austin.

(cont.)

line? Motherhood is made less stressful by girlfriends—power walking and power talking!

But it was when they talked late at night for hours that they really got close. When Rebecca turned fifteen she began to feel deeply insecure about her weight and developed serious issues with food. Rebecca recalls Hillary's understanding how she was feeling, but liked that she was not one of those pushy people. Rebecca says, "If I wanted to talk about what was going on with me [around eating disorders], she'd listen."

Eventually, Rebecca's disorder became so serious that she had to undergo outpatient treatment. When she was finally deemed well enough to travel, in the summer before eleventh grade, the two best friends embarked on a teen tour to Israel. They were inseparable. Although Rebecca thought she was being sly about her food problems, Hillary was keeping a close eye on her and noticed that Rebecca was barely eating. Hillary felt she couldn't just stand idly by and watch her friend slowly killing herself. So Hillary took the huge risk that Rebecca might never speak to her again and spoke up to

THE GIRLFRIEND CURE

According to a five-year study of depressed female teenagers by a professor of psychology at the University of
Southern California, girls felt their
friends did a better job of listening to
their problems, providing encourage-
ment, and conveying love and respect
than their boyfriends. Best friends
were a lot more supportive when a
girlfriend was going through a hard
time. Depressed teens described
their best friends as being kind and
outgoing, keeping confidences,
and listening patiently.

one of the counselors on the trip, explaining that Rebecca wasn't really eating. The staff called Rebecca's parents, and her mother asked to talk to Hillary. Rebecca was sent home without even having a chance to talk to anybody, being driven straight from the airport to the hospital.

Hillary called Rebecca from Israel, hoping she wasn't angry, and feeling terrible that she had caused her to be sent home. But Rebecca didn't blame her. She knew deep down that Hillary was only looking out for her, not tattling on her. As Rebecca recalls, "Hillary took a chance in terms of our friendship when she talked to the people in Israel. She stepped in at exactly the right time. That was when I realized people weren't as blind as I thought. Hillary was more of a true friend than ever. She really cared. Some people say they're your friend, but then let you do things in front of them that they know are bad for you. They're more concerned with themselves; they don't care enough to do anything. She cared so much about me that she put our friendship at risk to help me."

Rebecca now goes to college in Texas and Hillary is in school in Michigan, but even if the duo don't speak for months, when they do reconnect, it's as if they never left each other. Rebecca tells me, "I know that no matter what point in my life I might be at, I will always be able to call Hillary and we will pick up as if we'd just talked to each other. Hillary will always be one of my best friends."

Wellness and My Broad Squad

My girlfriend and the majordomo of my Broad Squad is Cathie Bennett Warner. Cathie is a kick-ass girlfriend with a throaty laugh, a zest for life, and a powerful professional mind. Several years ago, she came kicking and screaming to freewheeling San Francisco from buttoned-up Washington, D.C., leaving behind her beloved Colonial home and oxford shirts— not to mention all her best friends. In her mind, she was moving to the land of loony liberals where no one could talk about real issues. Her husband Chris was happily immersed in a new job as corporate counsel in a big company, fulfilling his dream of living in a city with a coastline and bridges. But Cathie, fearing she could never make friends with the left coast hippies, was trying to reinvent herself and make it on her own.

She was recruited to run Northern California operations for then-senator Pete Wilson's San Francisco office, and this allowed her to jump into a work frenzy. When it rains, it pours (and it always rains in San Francisco), so it's no surprise that three months into her exhausting but exhilarating 24/7 job, Cathie discovered she was pregnant. All was well until one night she fell into bed and discovered a very large lump on the side of her breast. Thirty-seven weeks into her pregnancy at age thirty-five, Cathie found herself on an operating table having a biopsy. A week later she was diagnosed with a very fast-growing form of breast cancer.

Cathie had survived an emotional move and a career reinvention, only to be told she probably wouldn't see her son's tenth birthday if she didn't act quickly. So first came ten days of induced labor to deliver a healthy baby, then a mastectomy, then six months of aggressive chemotherapy.

After her son was born, and she began treatment, her doctor introduced her to the cancer support community. On her first day, Cathie walked into a room full of diverse women all under forty: different political parties, ethnicities, even dress codes. But they all had one thing in common: breast cancer. Some had beaten it and some, like Cathie, were there to get well. In the "real world," Cathie would have closed herself off to many of these women because of their differing views. But almost immediately, their common experience turned this eclectic group of women into Cathie's new best friends, her inner circle, her lifeline to wellness.

Cathie learned cancer can be a great unifier. Many of the women in her group volunteered to come and take care of her new baby: cuddle, bathe, and rock the warm bundle of joy when Cathie was too sick from the chemotherapy to do it herself. Other women came to her home to scrub the bathroom, do the laundry, and just hang with her. So touched and thankful was she for their support, Cathie vowed if she beat the cancer she would dedicate herself to helping other women in the same situation.

Cathie made good on her word. As her health improved, she put her political abilities to work and, with others, began to organize fund-raising events, races, and survivor lunches to benefit breast cancer research. Besides Cathie's inner circle, other women in her group came out to support her, work for her, care for her, and join her in increasing breast cancer awareness. Some of the women Cathie thought she could never be friends with walked proudly next to her in San Francisco's first Race for the Cure.

With time comes perspective, and Cathie realized that her experience with breast cancer, as horrible as it had been, had opened her eyes to her true path, why the move from her great friends on the East Coast brought her to new girlfriends on the West Coast. It was clear to Cathie that she was destined to move west to meet these women who were to become her lifelong girlfriends—women she would never have become close with before, women she now credits with saving her life. Cathie feels in some small way she is giving back what they gave her by becoming a leader in bipartisan support for the research to find a cure.

As a postscript to this story, I recently attended a party at Cathie's home and there was celebration in the air: Christopher, her baby boy now fourteen, had just graduated from eighth grade and was awarded top honors for his class—and she was there to celebrate with him!

Cooking with Friendship

There isn't anything as devastating and debilitating for a woman as going through a divorce, especially after thirty years of marriage. Unless you are going through a divorce and are diagnosed with breast cancer at the same time, that is.

Ellen Rose had always been a take-charge type. When she made the decision to retire from her high-pressure TV producer job in order to carpool her young daughter, she did it with authority. Many career women turned full-time moms find that retiring from the outside world is not easy. So Ellen did what she wanted to do all her life: she followed her real passion and opened an all-cookbook bookstore she aptly named the Cook's Library.

Over the years she balanced her mom job and the operation of the bookstore—until she was hit with the double whammy of breast cancer and divorce. As her health and her marriage unraveled, Ellen fought to put more order and control in her life, as well as do something that brought her joy. So she began baking cakes. The rougher life got, the more cakes she baked. She discovered a Zenlike peace in following the recipe directions and took pleasure in having everything come out as it was supposed to (for once). Sometimes Ellen would bake a cake a day; while she was preparing for her double mastectomy, she would bake two cakes a day. All her friends knew how she was faring by the number of cakes she brought to the bookstore the next day to share with them and her loyal customers.

Ellen now says her girlfriends (aka the saints) were all that was holding her up during that rough period. They indulged her, listening to her tell her angry stories again and again and eating her cakes, even though they were all on diets. Never taking no for an answer, they made doctor's appointments for her, pulled her to the gym, and stood in her doorway until she finally relented and got dressed to go.

As Ellen's treatment began taking hold and she looked and felt better, she wanted to pay back her loyal girlfriends. Since it was her birthday and she was so happy to be allowed to celebrate it, she took her pack of girlfriends to Napa, California— land of gourmet delights. Ellen and her eleven girlfriends took over an entire bed-and-breakfast, quaintly tucked into the green hills and surrounded by vineyards, and had the time of their lives. Ellen toasted the true blue friends who helped her get healthy and happy.

Ellen can be found most days in the Cook's Library, and late at night she is happy to curl up in bed with a good cookbook—even though nowadays she bakes a lot fewer cakes.

A Celebration of Girlfriends and Wellness

One celebration of girlfriends and wellness I heard about came from Nancy Daly Riordan, a kind and beautiful woman who grew up in New Jersey and moved to Los Angeles as a young bride. Not only did Nancy manage to create an interesting West Coast network of girlfriends for herself, she also remained committed to the six women who had been her friends since grade school in New Jersey. Each year, Nancy made a point of getting her old friends together for a reunion, usually by flying to the East Coast, where the rest of her Broad Squad still lived.

But when their fiftieth girlfriend anniversary occurred, Nancy wanted to bring both of her worlds together for the first time. For this year's girl getaway, Nancy had all of her girlfriends from the east fly west to California, where she hosted a bicoastal girlfriend lunch for all of her friends in her elegant Malibu home. The magic was palpable. Her friends from both coasts had heard so much about one another that everyone felt as if they had known one another for many years. Putting faces to names and stories to girlfriends was a heartwarming game for the guests. Nancy beamed the entire day.

Within Nancy's Broad Squad of the original New Jersey Six was a dynamo lady named Kathy, who everyone loved to pieces. Several years earlier, after an incredibly brave fight, Kathy had succumbed to ovarian cancer. As Nancy raised her glass in Kathy's honor, tears streamed down the faces of friends from both coasts, some who felt the absence of such a dear friend and others who felt the loss of never having the opportunity to know her.

In Kathy's honor, Nancy invited Dr. Beth Karlin, the oncologist who nursed Kathy through the worst of her illness. She spoke to the emotional crowd about wellness and how important it is for girlfriends to take care of each other. Nancy's wellness luncheon was not only an important fiftieth reunion for an incredible group of women but a reminder of how precious our time together can be. This union of hearts and minds on both coasts was a tribute to girlfriends everywhere, and especially to the girlfriend who attended the party in spirit only, but was the inspiration for much laughter and many tears.

Chapter Three

Where the Girls Are: Girls' Night Out and Girls' Night In

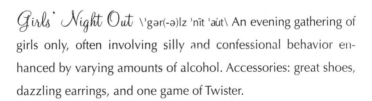

Girls' Night Out \'gər(-ə)lz 'nīt 'aùt\ An evening gathering of girls only, often involving silly and confessional behavior enhanced by varying amounts of alcohol. Accessories: great shoes, dazzling earrings, and one game of Twister.

GIRLS' NIGHT OUT with my Broad Squad is my therapy of choice: a time-out with a laugh track, an opportunity to share girlfriend secrets and come down from the stress and hype of a crazy week. Whether you get together in a restaurant or a bowling alley, a book club or a spin class, girls' night out is less about the activity, more about the after party. It's a time to get down, and get your groove, schmooze, dance, and share every dessert available—minus the usual obsession over calories.

As I travel across the country, I am inspired by the Girls' Night Out spirit that permeates the consciousnesses of goddesses everywhere. From storefront stitch-n-bitch groups to grrl communities online, we persistently find ways to reinvent the spinning wheel and weave friendship into our lives. I've met thirty-year-old women who have thrown down their poker cards and transformed their weekly ritual into a meditative yoga class. And I have met gal pals who are still going strong in their seventies. Like the Key Lime Sisters, who began their Girls' Night Out by meeting up at a local diner for coffee. So shocked were they when they all simultaneously ordered Key Lime pie (a sign?) that they decided right then and there that they would always be friends and would be known in their town as the Key Lime Sisters.

My Girls' Night Out group has taken the place of my extended family, who live thousands of miles away. I celebrate all the big hoopla holidays with them, but I've also called them at three in the morning in the midst of crisis, to have the gang of them show up at my door with bagels and cream cheese from my favorite 24-hour deli. And when I turned fifty and was so freaked out I didn't know whether to jump out of my own cake or hide in bed all day, my Girls' Night Out group surprised me with an incredible candlelight dinner— and what happens in Vegas stays in Vegas!

My favorite Girls' Night Out begins with a hike up the mountains before sunset. There's something about my Broad Squad discussing sex while we huff and puff our way through the wildflowers that keeps me laughing. After our trek, we settle in for a cool glass of white wine followed by a gourmet dinner at our favorite sushi hangout. No, it's not exactly swinging from the chandelier, but that's just the thing: for my Girls' Night Out I crave adult conversation (translation: no bull) with my smart, wise, witty, honest, nonjudgmental friends. I'm so not interested in scoring tickets to the hottest play in town, checking out a comedy club, or playing five-card

HANGOVERS: THE INEVITABLE AFTERMATH OF GIRLS' NIGHT OUT

Sometimes there's so much to talk about (and so much sake to drink!) that we forget how late it is and how early we have to be up for car pool or work the next morning. To that end, I've scoured the earth for my top Girls' Night Out hang-over cures. And here's a tip: Be on guard when you're in your hangover state. You are bound to say the wrong things, forget stuff, or press the Send button on an e-mail when you meant to erase it. So be careful. If you should, say, call your second husband by your first husband's name, your hangover will stay with you for weeks to come.

Girls' Night Out Hangover Cures

1. Keep a face mask, not a

stud poker. I want to talk—over cups of hot coffee, refilled over and over as our conversation changes course and deepens.

⸙ Spa Girls' Night Out ⸙

Girls' Night Out at the spa is a favorite for women who enjoy the finer things in life. While we may not be able to buy happiness, we surely can buy bliss. A deep tissue massage and an oxygen facial are the closest to nirvana any of us is likely to get. And who better to enjoy it with than your girlfriends? Get smooth skin and cute toes, relax in white robes, catch up on life, and listen to New Age music. I'm not sure why, but give a group of women some vanilla-scented candles, a masseuse, and a glass of wine, and we can easily develop a case of amnesia. What husband?

ℰ Aromatainment ℬ

Morgan Enloe's Bath Junkie store in St. Louis, Missouri, specializes in just this kind of bliss. Seven nights a week she runs what she calls an Aromatainment Girls' Night Out, where women can fall down a rabbit hole of delicious smells and tastes and excellent company. Slipping into Morgan's scented lair after hours, girlfriends sip apple martinis, compare notes on cosmetics, and chat.

And that's just the beginning! All the girls who step out here for the evening are confirmed twelve-step bath junkies. Martinis are nice, but

(cont.)

beer, in a bucket of ice by your bed. As soon as you open your eyes, apply the mask for five minutes. Then pry open your eyes so you can see the clock.

2. Hot shower. A number one Girls' Night Out accessory is a super-duper shower nozzle. Direct the spray and the heat to your neck and shoulders. Pinch your skin just to make sure you're still alive. Vow never to drink again.

3. Hangover hell can be reduced by a glass of water, an ibuprofen, a can of soda, and a sick day.

4. Eat breakfast. Forget the herbal concoctions. Try pure fat and carbs. Bacon, egg, and cheese on a bagel is the perfect post–Girls' Night Out breakfast. Tip: Get

(cont.)

someone else to make it for you or you may not survive the smell.

5. My girlfriend Mary swears by the girlie-girl hair of the dog: a lethal combination of vodka, tomato juice, Worcestershire sauce, Tabasco, and lemon juice. I never have, nor will I ever, try this but desperate times call for desperate hangover measures. And sometimes that means more vodka.

they're really here to do some serious sniffing. Each girl chooses from a variety of perfumes in a rainbow of colors, concocting whatever bubble bath, soap, or lotion her girlie-girl heart desires. After choosing a container, these ladies proceed to inhale their way through the display of bath paraphernalia: wax bead candles, crystals, colognes, perfume oils, and exfoliating salt scrubs. Love a strawberry scent but prefer a bright blue hue to match your bathroom tile? Anything is possible, and Morgan's seen it all! When you and your girl posse agree on the fragrance and products you want, the salesclerks mix, blend, and wrap your choices like party favors, while you savor the fantasy of a long soak in a hot bath.

Morgan says her Girls' Night Out is so successful because it's about girls relaxing together, creating soothing personalized scents, and enjoying a kind of therapy where they

---

CELEBRITY SECRET

Looking for a hilarious game that puts you and your girlfriends on a scavenger hunt for guys? The new Girls' Night Out celebrity must-have is a game called That Guy, which has been played by an A-list celebrity roster, including Julia Roberts, Drew Barrymore, and Charlize Theron. Hit the town and find real-life guys that match the cards you've been dealt.

P.S. The game doubles as a perfect divorce party favor.

---

control the outcome. But it's not all about sampling aromas and snapping up the food and punch. After the retail therapy is over, the girls snuggle into white terry robes and get down to business: slathered in ginger scrubs and sugar wraps, the verbal tête-à-tête begins, covering topics ranging from kids to husbands, careers to new waterproof mascaras.

Note that if it's racier aromatainment you're looking for, you can always hire outside entertainment. According to Morgan, one of the women dismissed the idea of a night of pampering and instead hired a male stripper for the

SPA NIGHT SECRETS

Plan your own Girls' Night Spa with one of these fun twists:

1. *Professional pampering.* Invite an expert from your favorite spa to perform facials or manicures for your group. Good party rates are often available.

2. *Much-needed massage.* Check with licensed massage schools and get a top student to experiment on you.

3. *Do-it-yourself beauty.* Ask guests to bring potluck for food, their favorite martini recipe and their best beauty product to share. Take turns pampering one another!

4. *The big splurge.* For a large Girls' Night Out, booking a suite at a hotel and splitting the costs may not be as

entertainment. Apparently he was quite a hit, and of course he left smelling great.

The Big D

One of the Girls' Night Out celebrations on my calendar recently was a divorce party for a girlfriend who got her walking papers and the deed to her very own house—all on the same day. We all met to cheer her on as she launched a life of new-found freedom and independence. If you have to go through a divorce, why not throw a party? Think of it as an official good-bye to Mr. Loser and a hello to the greatest girl of them all . . . YOU!

Multitasking Girls' Night Out

If you ask any girl to close her eyes and make three wishes, she would wish for diamonds, expensive shoes, and more time with her

> (cont.)
>
> expensive as you think. And you get a pool, a Jacuzzi, and room service to boot!

girlfriends. It's a tall order, but why not combine your fantasy life with your Broad Squad, and have a multitasking Girls' Night Out? Multitasking goddess gatherings make perfect sense for those of us who are out of time and out of our minds trying to do it all. We women need one admission price for a triple-header, and there are actually people who have figured out how to throw a goddess gathering and multitask at the same time.

ᘓ Belly Up ᘖ

Karen McLean of Washington, D.C., a dance teacher at the Arabesque Studio, hosts a perfect Girls' Night Out with a twist—literally. Listening to women always complaining about a lack of time for themselves, Karen brought together

THE DIVORCE PARTY

MENU: Serve cartons of french fries that your friend longed to eat but didn't because Mr. Loser thought her thighs were too big.

ATTIRE: Have the guest of honor wear her wedding dress (slightly shredded), and have her guests wear random bridesmaid dresses, before they get made into curtains.

ACTIVITIES: Hire a makeup expert to make her over.

GIFTS: Have the ex-bride register in a store for her "I'm single" gifts and get her started on her new home.

MEMORIES: Organize a scrapbook so that you can cut out all of the groom's pictures, thereby revising history and convincing your

a triple whammy of girlfriends, escapism, and exercise for suburban divas. Teaching an evening belly-dancing class for women of all ages and ethnicities, she invited everyone (the model thin to the Rubenesque) to stop by and strut their stuff to sexy music.

A core group of seven women who had never before laid eyes on each other—much less belly-danced—responded to the Girls' Night Out invite. At first, getting hips and breasts to move independently was a challenge, but eventually the dance became a form of therapy, not to mention a great giggle for all. Preening like Las Vegas showgirls in gold lamé outfits and dangly bracelets, they selected a winner in the categories of best rib cage, best castanets, and best earrings.

It took only a few classes before the women were coming less for the dance and more for the costumes and the laughs. Most of the women

(cont.)

girlfriend he never existed anyway.

PARTY FAVORS: Knives!

attracted to this evening were stressed-out professional soccer moms who originally joined to tighten their abs and surprise their husbands or boyfriends in the bedroom. But these women were surprised to find themselves suddenly in touch with their power centers, their womanhood unleashed as a result of the dance. So tight did the group become that they formed their own dance troupe called Ancient Rhythms and took their act on the road. The Girls' Night Out dancers have now become an official Broad Squad, seeing each other outside of class and developing close friendships.

Girls' Night In

Girls' Night In \ˈgər(-ə)lz ˈnīt ˈin\ Girls' Night Out without the makeup, shoes, and earrings. Accessories: PJs and a lot of attitude.

HERE COME THE CYBER BRIDES

There are certain truisms we women must accede to, facts about us that cannot be explained or altered. Here is one: There is no situation in which a woman becomes more psychotic than when she is about to become a bride. Maybe it's the overkill of ivory tulle and sugar frosting, but somewhere between deciding where you're going to seat your alcoholic aunt and whether to go with gardenias or ranunculus, you're bound to lose it. We all come out of the wedding planner's office one layer short of a triple-decker cake.

So it makes perfect sense to me that when a group of cyber brides met up at a wedding Internet site called TheKnot.com, they created an instant bond. With their French-manicured nails tapping out an SOS to

My favorite annual Girls' Night In happens on Oscar night, accompanied by one of my favorite girlfriends: my teenage daughter, AJ. From the red carpet preshow right through to the Best Picture Oscar, we dish over the divas, oohing over (or trashing) their hair, clothes, jewelry, and dates. We like to think of ourselves as Joan and Melissa Rivers, only funnier, kinder, and without the diamonds! To get the ritual started, we light the fire in the family room and load up on our favorite preshow snack combo: Brie and crackers with a chaser of peanut M&M's. Dinner itself is always special, but in truth, we rush through it so we get to the best part: the dessert of Häagen-Dazs coffee ice cream.

Chick Flick Girls' Night In

Of course you don't need the Oscars to have a Girls' Night In of your very own—you can throw a Chick Flick Girls' Night In any day of the year. Depending on your mood, there are several cinematic ways to go. You can laugh until you cry or you can cry until your eyes swell shut. You can choose a movie that will get your blood pumping (I mean full-on, self-righteous, justified *Norma Rae* kind of pumping), or you can choose something more lighthearted, where you cheer your heroine on as she comes from behind and wins the day (and usually the guy). No matter your Broad

(cont.)

their sisters (in the middle of the night because they couldn't sleep from all the stress), these women shared their horror stories and formed a Broad Squad that got them prepared for the walk down the aisle. So what to do once the weddings were over? They wanted to meet each other, of course! A group of twenty of them organized an evening at a bar in Washington, D.C., for a little après honeymoon gossip and the first Girls' Night Out for the Knotties.

Without revealing too many details, let's just say the party included beers, daiquiris, eighties music, and a few games of Pin the Hose on the Fireman. Wearing mock tiaras, fishnet stockings, and veils, these girlfriend "bachelorettes" bonded over alternative poetry writing: alternating one clean

(cont.)

word with one naughty word, that is. Secret language, indeed—the kind you keep secret from your new hubbie!

Squad's taste in movies, there is no better treat than homemade popcorn with extra butter and salt. And there is no better way to celebrate a Girls' Night In than in front of the VCR with you in control of the clicker, for once not having to explain to anyone (that is to say, a member of the other gender) why this movie has turned you into an emotional wreck or why you're busting your sides from laughter.

For women, the heart of a good flick is the relationship between a man and a woman, not an alien and a machine. Unlike the drug-trading robotic villains of guys' movies, Broad Squad heroines go after the real enemies of life: cheating husbands and evil bosses. As for the climax, well, art does imitate life. While guys are anticipating that big explosive release, breathlessly waiting for their enemy to be blown to bits, we look to the passion, the resolution of one on-screen kiss . . . and maybe a breathless "I love you" with an *Officer and a Gentleman* ending.

Girls' Clubs and Girls' Night In

Some of us are completely cool with penning our Girls' Night In on the calendar and coolly walking out the door for a night on the town with our Broad Squad. But others of us (and you know who you are) still feel guilty about leaving our families for "trivial" fun and frivolity that doesn't entail fund-raising for charity. Not true. Girls' Night In is as essential to your life as a fake Hermès is to your handbag collection. It may be the era of high speed (from the Internet to quick-dry nail polish), but that doesn't mean women don't need some time out for a night in with the girls. Still, old habits die hard; we may have a

KAREN'S TOP TEN FAVORITE CHICK FLICKS FOR GIRLS' NIGHT IN

THE HA-HAS: *Adam's Rib, A League of Their Own*

THE BOO-HOOS: *Breakfast at Tiffany's, Beaches, An Affair to Remember*

THE YOU GO GIRLS: *Norma Rae, All About Eve, Silkwood, Calendar Girls, Thelma & Louise, The Banger Sisters*

THE WE-LOVE-YOU-MEG-RYAN CLUB: *When Harry Met Sally, You've Got Mail*

DIVORCE, AMERICAN STYLE: *Kramer vs. Kramer, First Wives Club*

BEST LINE EVER IN A CHICK FLICK: "I'll have what she's having." (See, you're smiling!)

THE MISSED AMERICA PAGEANT

Who among us has ever been Miss America? More than likely, not many! I recently got an idea from a friend in Duluth, Minnesota, that is just a wonderful game to play at your PJ party. It is called the Missed America Pageant, and it celebrates all of us "average" women who missed out on being Miss America, but secretly dreamed of being her for just one day. Rather than a pageant of state representatives, the Missed America pageant celebrates the places you really call home. You and your girlfriends can represent anything from the local ball field to your child's kindergarten class. I make sure to include an evening wear segment (we dress up our PJs) as well as a talent competition. This, of course, is outrageously funny. Provide a basketful of boas, dramatic

hip-chick patina, but often we still feel guilty about leaving our families for time with the girls.

This neurotic inability to allow ourselves time for playdates has resulted in an explosion of book clubs—a chance to get together under the auspices of bettering ourselves. We all know that most of us look forward to our book clubs for two reasons: food and gossip. The book often becomes an opening to talk about our own lives, which are often more juicy and relevant than the lives of fictional characters.

Then I heard about a book club after my own heart. Rather than choosing a doorstop of a novel to read and discuss, the members in this group devoted the entire evening to discussing the articles in *People* magazine. Now this is a Broad Squad I could get into!

The *People* Magazine Book Club

Ann McCarthy and Jeri Bible began their *People* Magazine Book Club as a kind of no-brainer alternative to Tolstoy and Dostoyevsky. Every month at one of their homes in Montclair, New Jersey, twelve stressed-out professional moms (a bond trader, an interior designer, an actress, and a vice president in banking, to name a few) get together with their favorite junk food to gossip about the celebrities in the most recent copy of *People*.

They describe themselves as book club flunkies who tried but failed at the art of the book club. Finishing a book

(cont.)

hats, spike heels, and so forth, as well as noisemakers, kazoos, jump ropes. Your girlfriends can literally pick their talent out of the prop grab bag. Make sure your girlfriends state their platform (maybe they are hoping for the perfect apple martini rather than world peace). The one Miss America competition I skip? I have long spared my girlfriends from the swimsuit competition! The pageant is a surefire way to get your girlfriends laughing, and to appreciate all the wonderful things that make us all Missed Americas.

they often didn't like and then getting together to discuss it? Hello, who has the time? What these girlfriends had in common were hectic schedules, a need to connect with their Broad Squad, and a salacious interest in reading *People* as soon as the issue hits the stands. Once they discovered their mutual interest, the *People* club was born. Since then, they've solved some of Hollywood's hottest mysteries, including who designed Sarah Jessica Parker's Oscar gown and what J. Lo could have been thinking when she exposed her pubic hair line to the paparazzi. A burning issue was what was wrong with Teresa Heinz's hair color. The consensus: too many highlights! When they were done with that discussion, they played a game called Name That Body, which included strategically placed Post-it notes on an actress's face.

This reading group's only mission statement is that they have no mission statement. They do, however, have a slogan: "People who need *People*." As far as they are concerned, a lot of celebrities who show up on the pages of the magazine desperately need the group's help and advice. But the people who *usually* need them are off-limits when they're together.

Therefore husbands, children, bosses, and mothers-in-law are not allowed to call or page while the members are in session.

Of course the evening has its fill of girl talk and catty gossip. But often, among this close-knit group, the talk turns personal: work, divorce, marriage, kids. For Jeri, one of the club's founders, the members have been a true support system. Since she has really never been a "girl's girl," she didn't understand the importance of having other women in her life—until she went through a painful divorce at age forty and discovered that her *People* posse was actually a lifesaver.

Saturday Sisters

Sometimes the only excuse you need to get together with your Broad Squad is the fact that you want to be together. My girlfriend Anette, a beautiful southern belle, is the queen bee of a drop-in girlfriend day she calls Sister Saturday. At the drop of her designer hat, she invites women to come by and stay all day, or just drop in on their way to whatever obligations they have on the calendar. During these magical days, Anette serves up the three mandatory Cs of life: champagne, chocolate, and conversation. Her girls come as reliably as if they were going to church. There is even a Sister Saturday signature color: purple. That's why purple balloons roll around the pool area and purple hydrangeas always decorate the self-serve bar. Anette tells me she has many groups of girlfriends, but this particular group is made up of her best friends—her life therapists, her *Waiting to Exhale* companions.

In the beginning, Anette explains, the group was called Sista Saturdays, and was comprised entirely of African-American women. But now the Sista Saturdays have evolved to include Asian-American, Hispanic, and Caucasian invitees, selected for their girlfriend status alone. Ethnically diverse, these women connect with their minds, hearts, and souls. Along with the laughter and great chicken salad come some serious conversations. Like a sorority or secret purple society, they keep up-to-date on every detail of each other's lives.

Angela, a pretty girl in a blue suit, cries as she talks about the torment of her divorce. Carol, a transplanted New Yorker and a single parent, admits she doesn't know what she'd do for child care, car pooling, and emergencies without these women to support her. Her girlfriends are truly her family. Marlene echoes that sentiment when she walks in with her six-month-old adopted son. She is in her forties and single, and wasn't willing to wait any longer to start a brood of her own. Luckily, she has a network of friends to help her along the way.

But Sister Saturdays aren't all about the baring of souls; sisters provide news of a new outlet store, tales of shopping excursions, and reviews of the new hair salon in town. And there is even networking: Cathie and Jan huddle in the corner hammering out an idea for a women's group called Net-Walking. Not to be outdone by the guys' Wednesday golf outings, the women want the chance to exchange ideas and get some exercise, too.

The group gets smaller as we approach 5:00 P.M. Every once in a while a purple balloon pops in the late afternoon sun. When will the next drop-in Sister Saturday event take place? Anette smiles and says, "Everyone will start feelin' in their bones when they need another fix." Then she'll put out the word . . . and the girlfriends will come.

HOW TO HOST THE ULTIMATE PJ PARTY

Select a theme.

Throwing a fun and festive PJ party starts with a theme and a theme color. Some of my favorite girlhood memories involve the color pink. Pink twinsets, pink curlers, even pink Dippity-Do hair gel. The color evokes memories of the girliest of girls, like Sandra Dee, and even those classic tough girls, the Pink Ladies, from *Grease*. For my ultimate pajama party, the color pink is the ultimate inspiration. However, your inspiration may be Liz Taylor's violet eyes or a silver disco ball from Donna Summer's disco era.

Send out the perfect invitation.

In an era of e-mails and e-vites, it is important to remember the simple pleasure

No matter what activities we plan for ourselves, all we really want to do is talk. Laugh. Stay up. Talk. Eat. Drink wine. And then talk some more. About anything and everything: bosses, vacations, our childhood, guys, waterproof mascara, and world peace. Just sharing and connecting with one another. Talking our secret language is what we really want and need. Wherever you are with your Broad Squad, Girls' Night In or Out, here are the three basic rules: Always stick up for your friend, always call her right back, and always keep her secrets to yourself. And then just keep talking and relax. Being with our girlfriends is the one time we can really be ourselves—bad hair days included.

(cont.)

of opening a beautiful invitation or letter. Offer your pajama party guests that simple pleasure. Find a wonderful invitation—I've even sent a pair of pink PJs—and mail it off to your best girlfriends. The perfect invitation will set the tone to make this event extra-special.

Get comfy at the pajama party.

Once the pajama party starts, the first order of business is to get comfortable! Grab comfy Karen Neuburger pajamas and socks in pink or your theme color, and make sure your guests wear the theme color as well. There is nothing more important to a pajama party than a great pair of PJs that look as good as they feel.

Set the table.

Don't work too hard, but make it look like you did. When I get ready to decorate a table for my pajama party, I go to the local party store and simply "think pink"—pink bows, ribbons, napkin holders. These are easy to find and inexpensive, and provide a coordinated look. I even found a use for my old pashmina—it's the perfect luxury tablecloth.

Don't forget the food . . . and drinks.

The pajama parties of your youth always included pizza, an overflowing tin of popcorn, and lots of chocolate. Indulge in these favorites. One night won't kill you! Great-looking plates and glasses can dress up the simplest foods. I may be serving pink lemonade, but I serve it in pink martini glasses with little pink umbrellas to dress it up and make it special.

(cont.)

Load the Polaroid.

Some things you will do with your best girlfriends that you won't do in front of anyone else. I make my PJ girlfriends wear my now-famous girlfriend caps. I was inspired to create these fun caps because they are reminiscent of PJ parties from days gone by when girlfriends would wear rollers and cover their tightly wrapped heads in lacy roller caps. I made my own version of these caps for my girlfriends, and they must wear them at my PJ party. They also must pose for the camera wearing these hysterical creations. You can use this idea or set up your own photo ops using boas, floppy sunbonnets, or princess tiaras.

Make the memory, then save it.

After I collect a stack of hysterical Polaroids that capture the most fun moments, I encourage my girlfriends to create a PJ party page for their scrapbooks. (Even if they don't have scrapbooks, it is a fun activity that allows everyone to be creative.) An important aspect of throwing a PJ party is recording the memory and passing it on to future generations. For this reason, I also encourage journaling at the party. I love to see girlfriends writing together. It means that these fun times will never be forgotten.

Bring out the yearbooks.

What is more fun than scanning old yearbooks for bad hairdos, Coke-bottle glasses, and knee-high socks? A great part of spending time with girlfriends is looking back and sharing fond memories. Add a note to your invitations telling your girlfriends to bring theirs. Shuffle the yearbooks and share them. They are a great way to celebrate the past. They also make you thankful for the present—and your current hairdresser.

Let the games begin.

Every pajama party I throw includes games such as a trivia contest or Truth or Dare. You can depend on a game to break the ice and get everyone involved. Don't forget to award great inexpensive prizes for the winners of the games. For my pink-themed bash, I load up on pink bangle bracelets, nail polish, and even pink scrub brushes as prizes.

Load the DVD and CD

I want my girlfriends to feel free to dance and sing to their favorite songs. If they are having trouble getting inspired, I have a disco grooves CD or my eighties dance hits collection on hand for emergencies. I also love old movies and girlfriend stories, including *Thelma & Louise, A Summer Place,* and of course, *Grease.* John Travolta's swiveling hips never fail to make me melt. The *Grease* soundtrack has also been the background theme for some of my most memorable PJ parties.

The "Everything but Botox" Bowl

A day or two before my PJ party, I shop for the latest in beauty products. I gather all of these items, from pedicure sets to avocado hair treatments, into a huge pink bowl that everyone can dig into during the party. Some ideas for your bowl?

- ☐ Clay face mask
- ☐ Anticellulite foam
- ☐ Mani/pedi set
- ☐ Lots of pink nail polish
- ☐ Luxurious body cream
- ☐ Hairspray
- ☐ Hair gel

(cont.)

- ☐ Loofah
- ☐ Rollers
- ☐ Candles

A Good Dose of Friendship

The one PJ party must-have? A good dose of friendship, of course. There is nothing more important than celebrating good times with good friends.

Chapter Four
Chick Trips

Chick Trip \'chik 'trip\ A vacation for girls only, sometimes referred to as "Where the Boys Aren't." Often cleverly disguised as a cultural experience, a chick trip is really an excuse for women to combine uninterrupted laughter with intermittent shopping. Accessories: a tote bag filled with old movies, tissues, and your preferred hangover cure.

Bonding time with your Broad Squad (translation: a three-day sanity saver with a view) is the best way to bust out of town for a few days of new adventures, uninterrupted gossip, and as many Jell-O shots as you damn well please. Since *Thelma & Louise* set the bar for what can happen when girlfriends hit the road, you may be a little wary. But trust me when I say you don't need to commit murder or jump off a cliff to get some quality time with your Broad Squad. All you need is you and your road-raging girlfriends, a country-and-western radio station, and a spare tire that someone on board actually knows how to change. An authentic chick trip is one part sightseeing excursion, one part rehab . . . where the toxic buildup of bad boyfriends and dead-end jobs disappears in our rearview mirror like the road kill it is.

Back to Girldom

A girls' getaway is a secret club, like being cast on *Survivor* without all the vote-you-off-the-island garbage. No matter how old we are, women are always looking for a second chance at girldom: the feeling of our biological clocks ticking backward. And why not? In its purest form, a chick trip is a slumber party for grown women, without our mothers crabbing that it's time to go to bed. Some of my fondest memories are of being fifteen, at a PJ party, with half a dozen girls crowded into one bedroom, sleeping bags on the floor, makeup and nail polish everywhere. Now, all these years later (and I refuse to say how many), I think of the perfect chick trip as a Motel 6 clubhouse where we do exactly what we did as kids: Leave the lights on (all night), try on each other's clothes, talk about sex, give each other makeovers, and talk about sex some more. When on a chick trip, there are specific rules of indulgence. Krispy Kremes must be involved, and there must always be the option of wrapping up in big blankets and sitting outside at 5:00 A.M. to watch the sun rise. If you decide to haul yourselves out of your room for dinner, make sure you flirt with a CAW (translation: cute available waiter!). My friend Mary swears that according to the Broad Squad Rulebook, flirting with a CAW is not off-limits, even to a married girlfriend.

The Chick Trip as Therapy

When we're high on a chick trip, it's as if we've entered a parallel universe. The truth is there's no better cure for the depressed, overworked, and exhausted among us than a big-time

DEAR KAREN: AMEN TO NO MEN

Dear Karen,

Not to dis the men in our lives, or to look like we're running away from them, but trust me, we can all afford to live without them for a few days. Going away with just the girls is the difference between spontaneous retail therapy trips and a 24/7 scheduled vacation. And what is up with their resistance to ask for directions until we've practically gone around the world? Just make sure you tell your husbands and boyfriends that you're going, or they'll forget to feed the dog . . . never mind the kids.

Cindi

Durham, North Carolina

time-out under the stars. The travel time alone allows us to come down and decompress from the real world. With no outside responsibilities, we share a real intimacy that gives us new perspective on our lives, illuminating what we really want and need. Just like interviewing a focus group at a movie screening, we test our friends' reactions to our future plans, inviting their feedback as we shape and reinvent our lives. Women's lives are jammed with everyone else's issues and problems; it's no wonder we're exhausted, with all the hats we wear. We need a vacation without the hats—not to mention the makeup and the panty hose. It's tough to dwell on a lousy husband, a demanding mother, or an evil boss when you're laughing yourself silly while inhaling doughnuts in the back of a rented minivan. Plus, you'd be surprised how quickly you forget your troubles when you're lying around a hotel room, kicking back in silly pajamas singing "In the jungle, the mighty jungle, a wing, awack, a wing away."

Your Chick Trip Broad Squad

The most important element of organizing your Broad Squad trip is making sure you have a girl posse who will get along without irritating one another—or at least without killing one another. You need to assign the jobs of investigating cheap airline tickets, affordable hotel suites, restaurants,

SURVIVAL KIT ON THE ROAD

1. Swiss Army knife (now available in pink) with a beer/wine opener, nail file, scissors, and tweezers for the dreaded unibrow

2. A journal to jot down your thoughts and keep your Polaroids safe

3. Peppermint oil to wash down the hamburger grease and ward off the stench from groadie bathrooms

4. Dried fruit for the one girl who's always claiming hypoglycemic fainting spells (but only when it's her turn to pay)

5. One unbelievable trashy novel you've wanted to read forever . . . forever is now!

and a rental car. Next, poll everyone on their ideal agenda. What will it be? A dose of museums and galleries, a side trip to Graceland? A beach, a bar, a fake-bake tan, and some tequila? Of course the real differences become immediately apparent when you show up at the car or the airport with your luggage. There's always one girl with a small duffel that holds little more than sandals and a tube of SPF 30, another who awkwardly schleps in two gigantic Louis Vuittons stuffed full of shoes, every cosmetic product on the market, and maybe even a blender (to get a head start on the margaritas).

Once you've reached your destination, you need a treasurer (the one who keeps track of the moola), a photographer to document the event for posterity (silly pictures of sandy feet, leaping dolphins, and the girl with her head on the table from too much tequila), and at least one person who can read a map. Knowing everyone's requirements for food, sleep, and comfort ahead of time will prove crucial when you find yourself starving halfway to a rest stop, and all you have is a bag of Oreos and a full bladder.

Your Broad Squad has to include gal pals with a sense of humor and a taste for junk food, and at least one woman must come prepared with breath mints in her purse and toilet paper in the glove compartment. It's inevitable, by the way, that you're going to drink too much that first night and wake up with a headache. The next day you may be able to stay away from the booze, but in exchange you'll probably eat too much. So keep that Pepto-Bismol close by.

If you're thinking about curing your blues and blahs with a Broad Squad road trip, try this Travel IQ Test on potential travel companions:

1. **YOU REQUEST AN ETA. SHE:**
   a) thinks you want to know when she wants to EAT.
   b) hyperventilates
   c) has no idea there is an ETA. Isn't happiness the journey?

2. **SHE HAS TO USE THE BATHROOM:**
   a) every time you stop for gas or so
   b) every time you reach a new state or so
   c) every mile or so

3. **SHE SEES A HITCHHIKER AS:**
   a) a potential psycho
   b) a lost soul who's just looking for one last chance
   c) a potential husband

4. **IF YOU GET A FLAT TIRE, SHE:**
   a) gets out and changes it
   b) flirts outrageously to get some random guy to change it
   c) sells the car to get a newer one

5. **ON THE TRIP, SHE'S DETERMINED TO FIND:**
   a) every Prada outlet west of the Mississippi
   b) every cute gas station attendant west of the Mississippi
   c) the correct spelling of Mississippi

If she answered three out of five the way you would, she's probably a compatible travel companion. If she answered anything but *a* on question 3, leave her at home!

On the Road with . . . Me

Being a girl from the Midwest, where a long ribbon of highway is constantly calling out to you, I've always loved road trips. During my teenage years in Minnesota, my girlfriends and I would spend the weekends exploring new territory. With my skateboard in the trunk of my white Impala convertible (in case we discovered a great hill along the road), we would head due south, sometimes stopping for an impromptu picnic of salami and cheese by the side of the road. Our goal was to discover great resort areas around the lakes and new diners (for cheeseburgers and cold beer), have new girlfriend experiences (preferably with the sailing instructors), and create new Broad Squad rituals.

Hit the Road Rituals

It's our Broad Squad rituals that make our connections feel so special—as if we were the only pack of girlfriends on

Earth. Just getting out on the road with the top down resets our rhythm. We always start out kind of stressed and over-caffeinated. But not too long later, we've forgotten what day it is—never mind the hour. We start out looking kind of preppy, with a ponytail and some lipstick. Days later, our hair is messy, even dirty, and we wear no makeup. Call it grunge, without the tattoos. All of life's choices—marriage, job, wardrobe—fade into choosing whether to turn left or right at the stoplight.

Scuba Sisters

Each girlfriend group develops its own rituals. For Lisa Dohner, who works in the sales department at Sony, and her two close out-of-town friends, their chick trip is an annual scuba-diving getaway. Over the last ten years, Lisa, Lori, and Susie have explored the exotic waterways of Cozumel, Costa Rica, Belize, Honduras, Grand Turk, and Grand Cayman. They have left behind husbands, children, jobs, and just about any other responsibility you can think of to be together.

It is no accident this trio loves to scuba-dive on their annual getaway. Lisa and Lori met while they were getting certified.

Lori was Susie's best friend, and within minutes of meeting they became the Instant Soul Mates. Maybe it was their odd similarities. Outdoorsy girls who have a passion for adventure, this competitive trio likes to mountain-bike, ski, and perform other death-defying feats that don't make a lot of women's hit parade lists. Their similar interests—plus a love of pink drinks with umbrellas—really helps to draw them closer together.

"It's a more or less sacred vacation," explains Lisa. "We've seen each other through big transitions. Susie moved to Madrid a few years ago, I got divorced, Lisa had another child . . . and for the most part we support each other through e-mail and transatlantic phone calls.

THREE GIRLFRIEND GETAWAYS

1. *The femme fatale.* The Washington Terrace Hotel in D.C. has a package that takes women to the International Spy Museum and allows them to indulge in espionage fantasies. Breakfast delivered to an undisclosed location. Talk about secret code!

2. *Uptown girls just want to have fun.* This girl friends' weekend at the Four Seasons Hotel in Chicago features makeovers at Neiman's, tickets to *The Oprah Winfrey Show,* and a cooking class (code for wine and lots of laughs).

3. *Women's wellness retreat.* If you're looking for natural beauty, healthy walks, and activities like singing, chanting, journaling, and

(cont.)

yoga, the Sacred Space Wellness Retreat for Women outside of Cleveland, Ohio, may well be for you. Girlfriends explore the beauty of Kelleys Island, a migratory place for monarch butterflies.

When we're together on our annual girls' trip, we can really be ourselves. The way we dress, act, and talk feels authentic and real. But getting together is the equivalent of a religious experience. We really need that time to be in the same room, to talk all night, face-to-face, and let it all out. My bet is we'll probably keep diving together once a year until our eighties."

Ski Bunnies

For several years, my good friend Gerri and I have taken our daughters away on an annual ski week. Gerri and I have been friends since high school, and now our daughters are close friends as well. Making the drive up to the mountain remains part of the getaway ritual. Each year we shop along the way for treats to stock our cabin: homemade pies, yummy chocolate, fresh produce. The sound track of our trip is very important. We start off with "Happy Trails to You," and once we hit traffic, we pop in an Eagles tape and boogie in our seats. One year we were so stuck in traffic, we dragged our daughters out of the car, cranked up the sound, and danced on the highway to "Witchy Woman."

Of course, the ritual would not be complete without a stop at the outlet stores where the younger girls go off giggling to try on clothes, and the older girls hit the home furnishing stores. Loaded down with shopping bags and usually high from retail therapy, we arrive at our cabin late, light a fire, and cozy up in our warm socks and pajamas to share a chick flick.

No one is ever in too much of a hurry to hit the slopes the next day. Our daughters usually make it onto their snowboards long before their mothers strap on their skis. After a couple of runs (why push it?) we meet the girls for a great outdoor lunch at the top of the mountain where even an ordinary hot dog with everything on it tastes gourmet. After an obligatory run or two, Gerri and I retire to the lounge for some hot toddies and long conversations, commiserating about how fast our daughters are growing up. This chick trip is important to me not only because Gerri and I share Broad Squad time together, but because we've watched our daughters

DEAR KAREN

Dear Karen,

  Even though we women are all perfectionists at heart, we don't need to be able to afford two weeks in a villa in Tuscany to enjoy ourselves. Of course it's wonderful to travel to decadent, ooh-la-la destinations. But we can also take a day off at the beach, visit a day spa with our girlfriends, or hit a local motel for the night, and still reap the benefits of a girl posse getaway. We all put such pressure on ourselves to be flawless. The trick is to let go of all expectations and grab the time you can with the women in your life who nurture you. Life is too short not to jump at the chance to spend quality time with the women you love.

Sara

Boise, Montana

grow into young women over the years. I know I'll never be able to drink hot chocolate with marshmallows and peppermint sticks ever again without reminiscing about this very special ritual.

The Glam Girls

There are many ways for your Broad Squad to take an annual sabbatical together. Leslie Ann Butler is a native Oregonian, a portrait artist in her forties who celebrates her girlfriends with an annual getaway at her beach house in honor of the summer solstice. The summer solstice, which symbolizes renewal, comes around the third week of June, when the day reaches its maximum length. Every year for the last four years, Leslie and her core group of girlfriends have gathered to welcome the summer and renew their friendships. It's a time for eating, talking, and too many margaritas sipped in an oversize hammock. The unofficial nickname of this eight-woman group is the Glam Girls, named for the year they formed a spontaneous chorus line, complete with high-kick choreography, and lip-synched to Bette Midler's "I'm Beautiful."

> ### GIRLFRIEND TRAVEL TIP
>
> To keep pickpockets away, fasten a safety pin across the opening of your pants pocket on the inside. Leave just enough room to pull out your billfold with some effort, but not enough for a quick hand to lift it.

They indeed are a glam and varied group. Among them are a lawyer, a financial adviser, a newspaper columnist, and a fund-raiser. Not that you'd know it: time stops during the Summer Solstice Weekend, as if the outside world is gone. It's just Leslie Ann and her girlfriends, with no outside interruptions. As is true of any great chick getaway, this group has its own rituals.

"We enact a ceremony," Leslie Ann explains, "where each woman tells the other what she means to her in very specific ways. Each woman in the room is praised and thanked for what she has given her girlfriends over the past year, and I'm talking specific details. Then we all make wishes for ourselves, write them down on paper, and throw them into the fireplace. Like a blessing, the smoke takes our paper wishes to the heavens. Then we offer each other little symbolic gifts; funny, serious, or intimate. Some we make, some we find. If the weather cooperates, we build a bonfire on the beach and complete the ceremony there. Then we dress up in lacy finery and indulge in a gourmet meal around the table.

"Our secret language is that we have no secrets. When one of us has a problem, we approach it as if we all have a problem. And we spend a lot of time providing each other with solutions. A glass of champagne under a starry sky and another toast to our summer solstice girlfriends."

Broad Squad Alias

Here's the thing that guys don't get. Every once in a while, we women want to crawl out of the skin we were given and take on another woman's persona. For a day or a week, we'd all like to live out the fantasy of being a pole dancer, of course with a fake ID, becoming the person we were clearly and unfairly not meant to be. The chick trip is the perfect place to meet people you will never ever see again. So if you're married with children, and your secret desire is to be a stockbroker or a hat check girl or someone with a foot fetish, now's the time. Just stroll into that bar filled with stories, none of them true, and dig the response. Your Broad Squad will be there to protect you—or to rush you out the back way should you get in over your head.

Las Vegas Bachelorette Getaway

One of the most popular Broad Squad getaways is to take a future bride away for her last weekend of freedom. I heard about one pediatrician who was about to say "I do." In order to say good-bye to the single life, she left her lab coat behind and escaped with her girlfriends to the clubs on the Vegas Strip. When the bride and her bridesmaids got to the room, her maid of honor broke out the body glitter while her soon-to-be sister-in-law handed out T-shirts with bachelorette dares printed on them in black Sharpie pen.

Then the real chick trip began. A white veil was brought out for the bride to wear, and the rest of her entourage was handed push-up lingerie and black eyeliner pencils. Decked out like the women they were raised never to be, they proceeded to their club of choice, where they ran into just one hitch: a line in front of the entrance a mile long. One of the bridesmaids palmed the bouncer a stack of bills (which he never counted, being too busy staring at her trashy lingerie). Someone passed out shots, which the bride downed immediately, to her Broad Squad's surprise. They'd never seen their friend drink, much less do a shot! The women all danced in a circle, bees around the queen bee. At some point someone dared the tipsy bride to stick her hands down some guy's pants, but thankfully she wasn't *that* drunk.

At three in the morning, everyone was dizzy and hung over and their feet hurt—secret language for "time to go home!" The only problem was that no one could find Dr. Bride—she had left the building. Many Tylenols, glasses of water, and worried phone calls later, they found her just where a doctor should be: at the hospital. Turns out those first-time shots (vodka, not penicillin) had left her feeling woozy. She self-diagnosed dehydration and set off for the nearest hospital for an IV and some sleep!

In spite of that debacle, the bride remembers the weekend fondly. "It was the most fabulous send-off by my girlfriends I could ever imagine," she gushes. "I loved the fact that for once in my life I could be someone completely different from who I am."

Wild Women on Wine

If you don't want to go quite that far to be wild, but you're still willing to take some risks, you can really let loose on a girl adventure. For whatever reason, even if we don't assume an alias, we're different women on the road than we are at home. The rules that apply in a candy-red convertible do not apply anywhere else on the planet.

Some wild adventures are wild in name only, like one fabulous girlfriend getaway in Napa Valley called Wild Women on Wine. Their mission statement? "We come in all shapes and sizes, but we're all of one mind." On the day I met them, fifty women had gathered together on a girls' getaway to taste wine, eat cheese and chocolate, and bond with other women. That's women only—and in case you forget, the sign outside the winery where they gather reads NO STINKY BOYS ALLOWED. It's like the clubhouse you had as a kid, but infinitely better for one reason: there's wine!

The architects behind this business are best friends Shanin Martin and Cathy Walk-Nelson. Six years ago they took their own wine-tasting girls' getaway, and it changed their lives. On their first trip, they laughed and cried so much, they couldn't wait to go again. By the third year, they had invited friends, rented a minivan, and with one girlfriend selected as their designated driver, proceeded to visit one winery after another in search of that perfect Chardonnay. Along the way, they were blown away by the beauty and the magic of being together, and began wondering how they could turn their love for girl getaways into a business.

Years later they did just that. Wild Women on Wine is now a tour company offering wine-tasting chick trips for women. One of the reasons Shanin and Cathy have been so successful is that they know how to get down and be girlie-girl silly. On one of their favorite adventures, Shanin says they "got into the van with a group of women and gave everyone glow sticks. It was pitch black out, so we looked like a traveling electric light show. We took out our kazoos, harmonicas, and tambourines, sang at the top of our voices, and ate jelly beans. It was a group of grown-up girls acting silly and crazy." Sounds like a good time to me! For more information, you can check out their website, www.wildwomenonwine.com.

CONFIDENTIALLY YOURS . . .

Teresa Delillo began her travel service, Menopausal Tours, after she got divorced and her therapist encouraged her to travel. Not having any girlfriends, she joined a group of women from work who were going to Vegas for the weekend. She ended up having such a good time that she decided to open up to the world of women travelers, so they wouldn't feel so alone. This year, Teresa will accompany you to Tuscany, Savannah, or New Mexico for hot air ballooning.

Reentry

Whether you're out on the road discovering yourself and America, honoring your friend the bride, or meeting for an annual reunion in your home, the most difficult part of a chick trip is reentry back into real life. There is nothing worse than that dreaded sound of your key in the door with nothing behind it but endless problems: bundles of bills, a dripping faucet, a refrigerator you forgot to clean. Here's my trick to deal with real life. I take a little garbage bag filled with the remnants of my chick trip, and I'm talking trash—lottery tickets, an empty doughnut box, ponytail elastics, diner receipts—and tuck it away in a little corner drawer of my desk. That way, when I need a few days of Broad Squad time, I can take a look and immediately start planning the next trip. The sooner, the better.

Chapter Five

Girlfriendship at Work

Girlfriendship at Work \'gər(-ə)l-, frend-ship ət 'wərk\ The way we make it through the day. Ex: "I'm not supposed to cry at the office; please meet me in the bathroom."

If women can sleep their way to the top, how come they aren't there?

—ELLEN GOODMAN

IF I DIDN'T have my girlfriends at work to commiserate with, I would have gone certifiably insane by now. I have girlfriends in my Broad Squad who are total workaholics, gal pals who define themselves by their work. Driven, ambitious, with a very extensive shoe collection, they live for the deadlines, the promotions, and client dinners at hot new restaurants—on their expense accounts, naturally. But not every girl is an obsessive career type. I have other girlfriends on my team who work to pay the bills in order to support their real passion (that is, scuba-diving, painting, and traveling), waiting for their big break, or for some fabulous guy in the oil business . . .

In the meantime, all of my girlfriends, no matter the level of their passion for work, keep a good attitude. After all, with the perks of a weekly paycheck, daily gossip, and free Post-its, working can be a great sideline while you're waiting for your real life to begin! I also know women who work from a home office in self-owned businesses. Their perks are the ability to stay in their pajamas all day and walk the dog at lunchtime. And then there are those friends of mine who work at home, in the home. Anyone who doesn't consider chasing after a toddler (while trying to keep a house organized, a family fed, and the car pool on schedule) as real work needs to be sent back to the century (and planet) he came from.

No matter why you're working, most of you are working girls. And where there's work, there's a need for a professional brand of the Broad Squad to get us through our day. These are the girlfriends who keep us juiced about our professional path, and who offer up advice, pep talks, or Snickers bars when life at the watercooler gets rough.

My experience from working with many women over many years is that as office girlfriends, we watch each other's backs in perfect harmony. We excel at the simultaneous eye roll, not to mention the art of sneaking a Krispy Kreme from the conference room. Here are my top ten professional picks for a professional Broad Squad.

Top Ten Broads to Have on Your Professional Squad

1. The Stall Girl. When you're ready to break down and cry in front of the boss, she's your girl! She will wait for you in an empty bathroom stall and do the silent-scream thing with you. Her motto: Better anger than tears. But if you can't hold back the waterworks, she'll never let you return to your desk with puffy eyes.

2. The Gossip Girl. She's the one who knows everything about everyone in the office, including birthdates, shoe sizes, and preferred color of paper clip. You need her for the lowdown on your coworkers and your boss—including whether the blonde you saw him with last week is his daughter . . . or not.

3. The Random Know-It-All Girl. This friend has a world of knowledge at her well-manicured fingertips. Among her tidbits are hot stocks on Wall Street, hot brokers, and the new hottie that's just been secretly hired. She's always up on industry happenings, and in particular, knows who's on the guest list.

4. The Foodie Girl. This girl knows every restaurant within thirty minutes of the office, including drive time, best route, special prices, off-the-menu dishes, and regular customers, along with what days they can be found at what table. She is also an expert on take-out! A necessary friend to have when you're sleeping at the office to meet a deadline.

5. Geek Girl. She knows enough about your computer, fax machine, copy machine, and telephone system to pull you out of the "I am so screwed" nightmare while you are waiting for the tech guy to show. If your Palm Pilot crashes, she's the one who can save your Rolodex—thereby saving your life. She may wear funny shoes and glasses, but you're nice to her anyway.

6. Snack Sister. Different from Foodie Girl. This girl could care less about the restaurants. She's all about the snacks. An indispensable member of your professional Broad Squad, she will rescue you from PMS and hypoglycemia, sharing both your misery and her Twizzlers any time of the day or night.

7. First-Aid Friend (or Miss Red Cross). She has everything from Kleenex to Tampax to a shoulder for crying on. Looking for an extra pair of hose? Red polish to touch up your manicure? She has what you need. This

Girl Scout is prepared for any disaster. If there's a blackout, head toward her desk. She'll be the only one in the office with a flashlight.

8. Designing Diva. Your own personal stylist, she will be the first to show up in this season's sunburst yellow. She'll know turquoise jewelry is back (again), that denim is very in for casual Fridays and date nights, and that when it comes to your walls, orange is the new white.

9. Happy-Hour Honey. This girlfriend is the instigator for those afterwork get-togethers, and she can always find (or create) a convincing reason to meet at the bar. You should go with her once in a while just to see who shows up, but try to stay at least one drink behind her; you know she's got a camera hidden in that purse, and she's not afraid to use it.

10. After-Hours Sister. When you're on a deadline, she's the one who brings you your favorite salad at midnight, with your favorite dressing and the crunchies on the side.

Personally Speaking

The one work problem we girlfriends have—and let's just say it out loud—is that we can be just this side of wimpy. Guys pound their chests and aggressively push their way into the A-list projects. Without a moment's hesitation, they blow off their anger in one gigantic primal scream behind closed doors, and then they're done. Women, on the other hand, take everything personally and can obsess over an offhand remark for days. We allow our hurt feelings to get in the way of that promotion or raise because too often we're not able to compartmentalize, to separate business from pleasure. Instead we rely on Stall Girl to do the silent-scream thing or Snack Sister to dole out Hershey Kisses. In the end, we're still not professionally satisfied.

The upside is that we take things more personally because we are beings of many parts and that's how we relate to the world. At the office, we talk about our marriages, our mammograms, and our mentors—and that's all before coffee. Having such personal relationships can be a double-edged lipstick for us. It's time-consuming to be walking on

BROAD SQUAD PROFESSIONAL ADVICE

1. Meetings in the bathroom are often more effective than meetings in the boardroom.

2. If you're going to schmooze, do it with the boss's secretary. She or he is the one with the power.

3. Negotiations for a raise should be done after lunch but before menopause.

4. Don't be a clock watcher at work—just set the alarm.

5. Everyone's stash drawers are fair game after hours. Learn to share!

those hormonal eggshells. On the other hand, when times are tough, we can count on support from our professional Broad Squad to get us through our various crises. Unlike men, praise isn't the only thing we're after. We're all about who we are—and who we are is a triple combo of work, family, and friends. That's why we always need a professional Broad Squad to provide us with free therapy and professional advice.

Pajama Game

When I began my career thirty years ago as a young bride and mother in Duluth, I wasn't looking for passion. I needed a job that would feed our family and put my husband through school. So, after meandering through the cashmere department (four-ply, rainbow colors) of the most prosperous and trendy store in town, I strolled into the personnel department to see if there were any positions that involved shopping and a weekly paycheck. The only credential I possessed for the world of fashion was that I loved to shop. Correction—I was born to shop. So it is truly one of my life's most amazing serendipities that I was able to convince the HR woman to give me the job of sportswear buyer for their twenty-store operation. Of course I had not a clue what a sportswear buyer did, but the job description sounded like the job I was made for: shopping till I dropped and getting a paycheck at the end of the day.

My coworker and designated trainer Diane turned out to be cool and distant, who at first showed me nothing but her perfectly arched eyebrow of disdain. But by complete accident, one day we ended up sitting next to each other at the lunch counter of our favorite haunt, Snyder's Drugstore. That day, with egg salad oozing out of our sandwiches (so attractive!), we had our first conversation. Balancing on those dinette stools with pieces of egg between our teeth, we discovered we had a lot in common. Back at work, Diane then introduced me to her friend Mary, an influential flagship store manager, and the three of us became the Office Broad Squad: an unbeatable retail fashion team.

From that day on, we were like a sorority. We traveled, schemed, and triple-teamed even our toughest vendors to negotiate the best deals and fastest shipping. We were invincible; nothing got past us. We had every angle of the office covered. Just like Stepford Wives, we began to look alike: same oversized tote bags slung casually over our shoulders, same Candies shoes (which gave us our swing and swagger), and same Charlie perfume (we all loved the song and the ad). We looked like three cookie-cutter working girls, but the best part was that we were in complete control.

Our secret club was so tight, each of us even had our own Broad Squad assignments: I was in charge of the M&M pick-me-ups (Snack Girl); Diane and Mary (Random Know-It-All Girls) provided emergency makeup and accessories in case of a cute male sighting. To show you the power of girlfriends at work, we all ended up not only successful, but raising our daughters together; to this day, our girls are friends. We shared staplers and child care, traded clothes and stocks. Diane and

Mary became my numero uno professional Broad Squad, and the very best Stall Girls—ever!

Pajama Mama

When I launched my business, my youngest daughter AJ was only a toddler. So to raise her while kicking off my line of boyfriend pajamas for girlfriends, I blended baby food on one side of the kitchen and sewed inseams on the other. When everyone got tired of mashed pea stains on the fabric, I eventually rented out a little space where my four female employees and our children worked and played all day. One woman, Misty, who was drastically underpaid, came to work for me only because her fiancé lived in my area and she was desperate for a

HOW TO HELP YOUR GIRLFRIEND REINVENT HER PROFESSIONAL SELF

* Help her update her résumé by reminding her of her accomplishments.

* Role-play the interview with her. Throw some tough questions at her, and prepare her as if she's entering a professional boxing match.

* Drill her on articulating her skills, so she's ready to talk about how her strengths dovetail with the company's needs.

* Constantly tell her how fabulous she is. Because she is!

* Dress her appropriately. Take away her black

(cont.)
miniskirt and lend her your boring but comfortable pumps. No black eyeliner!

job. The other woman was my husband's secretary, whom I stole from right under his nose. Literally, he went looking for her one day and discovered she was working for me . . . you snooze, you lose! (Richard still has not forgiven me.) Our children were hilariously distracting; very little got done between the laughter, the gossip, and the diaper-changing. On the first Monday of every month, we would hold a sample sale in our little work space, and all of our friends would come with their children to shop and eat a potluck lunch.

Despite our frivolity, the distribution of my pajamas was picking up speed, flowing into every major department store. Then came the day that changed my life forever. Over the loudspeaker came an announcement for me to answer the phone: Oprah was on the line. Thinking it was a prank call, I laughed and teased and cajoled her to tell me who it really was—at least until I shut up long enough for her to speak. Hearing that distinctive voice I realized, "Oh my God! It really *is* Oprah!"

Before I almost passed out, I recall her telling me she had been sent a pair of my pajamas and had thought they were very comfortable, so she wanted to order them as Christmas presents for all of her friends. Telling her that was no problem (a complete lie), we all scrambled to unearth bolts of fabric to make up the pajamas in record time. Once that mission was accomplished, Oprah called again. Now she wanted us to be on her first ever "Favorite Things" show, supplying pajamas to every member of her studio audience.

The rest is a blur. I remember someone holding open the door to a limousine and then being escorted into Oprah's greenroom. I recall sitting on the TV set in my pajamas, feeling that this must be happening to somebody else. Women who saw the show that day went scrambling out to the malls, fighting over pajamas I had once sewed in my kitchen. Oprah made my career, and to this day I still consider her one of the best girlfriends anyone could ask for. By that I mean she is a girls' girl, somebody who gets out there, walks the walk, and supports other women in their dreams and accomplishments.

SECRET DESK STASH INVENTORY

Sweet 'N Low, Altoids, flat shoes, extra panty hose, change for the vending machine, M&Ms, Broad Squad's phone numbers, a vase for flowers, the florist's number for ordering your own, a can of Slim-Fast, a restaurant menu from the place that delivers, a makeup mirror, a clean blouse in case you didn't make it home last night, Advil, a thesaurus, three o'clock music (fast, sing-alongable, and danceable), Tampax, Kleenex, perfume, a security blanket or teddy bear (well hidden), an unflattering picture of your boss taken at the holiday party (also well hidden), a picture of your dream promotion motivator (a BMW, the Caribbean vacation, George Clooney).

Office and the Single Girls

Now that my business, like my daughter, is all grown up (AJ is now in college), we employ a full staff. I first took notice of the different cultures in my office when Jenna Lowe, one of my newer KN Broad Squad members, put up a picture of the actor Orlando Bloom. When I first heard his name, I thought he was an orchid. But Jenna and the rest of the younger women in the office think he's the bomb.

Since they spend so much time at the office, many of the single gals look to their work environment for their social life as well. I notice how quickly they bond: carpooling, discussing office politics at the watercooler, laughing about their weekend dates. While I grab a sandwich and a fashion magazine at lunch, they go for a

walk on the bike path and munch on an après-exercise gra-
nola bar. While I listen to a little Frank Sinatra and some
Tina Turner, they spin their alternative music, actually voting
on what gets played on a certain day. At four o'clock the girls
in the art department all get together for tea, and on Friday
night they leave the office all made up—for where, I'm too
old to know!

Networking

For all the information out there about the perfect black
dress and the latest indelible lipstick, you'd think someone
would help us get a clue about women's problems in the
workplace. What we need is some working girl wisdom that
goes farther than telling us not to get busy with our boss on
top of the Xerox machine. (Duh!)

These days networking is about getting to know
other women on a personal level. I love my networking
friends. Not to diminish our motives or sincerity, but we
use each other in the nicest of ways. Mutually symbiotic
and supportive, we keep an eye out for each other and pro-
mote one another whenever possible. Although our lifestyles

THE LADIES

There's a networking group called the Ladies made up of nine women between the ages of thirty-two and fifty-two who live and work in New Jersey. Their mantra is "leap, and the net will appear." Last year each member brought a decorative angel inscribed with her name to their meeting. While one member read a poem, the women passed their angels around the circle. At the end of the poem, each woman found herself holding the name and angel of her new cheerleader. That personal angel is her special support person for the coming year, the one who will go beyond the call of friendship whenever needed. What a reason to believe in angels!

are different—married, single; kids, no kids; gay, straight; city girls, country girls—what we have in common is that we are women in the business world. And that fact is a great equalizer.

I have a tight networking circle that meets on Sunday mornings for power hikes (aka walks to brunch). Huffing and puffing up a mountain, we discuss professional concerns and issues as seriously as if we were sitting in a board meeting. Picture eight women in black spandex and oversized sweatshirts, climbing the trails while analyzing the stock market. Cute, huh?

No networking power hike is complete without full disclosure of our more personal matters: guy stuff, latest diets, and fashion trends. We race through hot health store buys and family dramas so we can cut to the good stuff: gossip! If someone sends out an e-mail suggesting a power hike, that's translation for "one of us needs the advice of her networking Broad Squad."

Crave

What do women want? We want love, a kick-ass job, and as much time with our girlfriends as our spa schedules permit. With our crazy lives, it's often our friends who fall off our to-do lists. We need a way to combine our responsibilities with our girl time, preferably while wearing pajamas. Melody Biringer may have found the way.

Melody, a so-called start-up junkie from Seattle, is such a bundle of workaholic energy, she had to schedule time away from the office to relax and bond with her friends. Having begun a personal services business, she spent a lot of time transporting her army of massage therapists and facialists to house parties and bridal showers. Over and over again, she heard how women were tied to their jobs and their kids and weren't spending enough time with one another.

A SALUTE TO OUR HAIRDRESSER

One of the most universal kinds of girlfriend networking takes place at the beauty salon, and I wanted to honor the hairdressers in our lives who play such an important role. Never is our secret language so fluid and open as when we sit under those dryers, strips of hair wrapped in silver foil, reflecting upon our lives. Maybe it's the chemicals in the dye, or the vulnerable feelings we get as our protective tresses are trimmed and cut. Maybe it's the soothing calm we feel being surrounded by so many fashion magazines, or the luxury of being served water with lemons or cappuccino with extra foam. But for some reason, with our hairdresser, we feel very exposed. Whether we're blonde or brunette, she is

A Crave Party is Melody's answer to working women's need to indulge themselves with champagne, food, and great conversation while meeting other professional women—in their pajamas. In order to increase their relaxation time, she took a page from the speed-dating book and paired women in a thirty-second speed-networking interview. If each found the other interesting as girlfriend material, they were given each other's numbers.

Melody's whole goal was to get women together, out of their business suits, and into their PJs, so they can destress and relax. How much fun is it to reinvent yourself while you're indulging in foot treatments, facials, and henna tattoos?

Ferry Tales

We women connect so instantly with each other, it's like someone touches us with a magic wand and suddenly we're lifelong friends.

(cont.)

our chief therapist and adviser. And for that, we salute her!

Why else would we find ourselves sharing intimacies over the copy machine with a woman we've met only minutes before? That magic can happen anywhere, anytime. While running at breakneck speed, we manage to connect with one another—even if it's on our way to work.

That's what happened to six women who met five days a week on the 8:15 A.M. Staten Island Ferry from St. George to Manhattan. For the better part of ten years, this group of very diverse women would hightail it to the ferry's aqua-and-white powder room, using its double mirrors and fluorescent lights to get ready for work. With bottles of makeup and hair gel spread all over the counter, they'd fix their hair, put on their faces, and talk about everything: marriages, kids, men, movies, dreams. No subject went untouched, despite the limited time frame and busy locale.

Elizabeth Ferris, an administrative executive for the New

THE GLIN PARTY

My girlfriends in New York all worked in the same office and we called ourselves the GLIN girls, for Girls' Life in a Night. Because we were all married or had serious boyfriends, when we saw each other we crammed every possible girlie thing you could do into one night. We'd start with a manicure and pedicure, go to Loehmann's for shopping, grab some dinner, and then head out for drinks. It would be a whirlwind night that we would pay for the next morning at the office.

York City Ballet, was a latecomer to the Staten Island Ferry powder room but was immediately accepted into the group. She describes their ride to work as six women living in suspended animation. By that, she means they were no longer fundraisers, accountants, fashion designers, and social workers, they were an extraordinary group of supportive girlfriends discussing and laughing about the real world of relationships, career aspirations, and the benefits of waterproof mascara. Without interruption, they lived in a surreal commute. They would talk seriously about their lives, all the while painting their nails and (yes) even shaving their legs.

As the self-described most reserved member of the group, Elizabeth was amazed at the support she received from her work Broad Squad as she went through the agonizing process of adopting her baby son Nicholas from the Ukraine. "But," she quickly adds, "that was just my drama." Valerie Campbell didn't always ride the ferry. When she first came to New York she lived in a battered women's shelter with her children. Irma Indicia had been molested as a child, and now with the support of her ferry group this mother of four aspires to be a fashion designer. Rachel Francis has three children and works as a therapist in a foster care agency. The ride to work is her calm before the storm.

All of the women had issues they were dealing with, and every morning they could look forward to a half-hour therapy session with their ferry friends. So unique was their story that Hollywood paid them a casting call. A documentary was made about their friendships called *Ferry Tales*, which in

PASSION PARTIES

The coolest girl I've ever met with an alternative but legitimate job is Pat Davis, who runs a business called Passion Parties. She travels the country getting bands of girlfriends together to talk about—and learn about—sex. She says that usually the "women get together, and after some nervous giggling and a few stone-cold looks of terror, one will begin to open up about her sexual pleasures and problems. The other women are usually astonished they feel the same way!" After the girlfriend comfort level rises and the heated discussion ends, Pat passes around confidential order forms for interesting books and toys. Now, that's a party I'd like to be invited to!

2003 was nominated for an Academy Award for Best Documentary. Yes, all of them flew to the Hollywood premiere, still not believing that their group of girlfriends was the toast of Rodeo Drive.

And the ferry tales continue. "Today," Elizabeth tells me excitedly on the phone, "my group is going back on the ferry again, but this time for pleasure: my son Nicholas's christening. I could not have done it without them. And I can't wait to see them all."

Sister Friends

You've really hit the mother lode if your sister also happens to be your very best friend. Although many of us refer to our girlfriends as sisters, Sarah and Jennifer Jaqua are real-life sisters. They're also the brains behind a very popular gift called the Beauty Parlor Kit. You've seen them on the shelves:

a silver tin with pink etching, filled with everything you need to create your very own at-home girlfriend spa night.

As children, these best friends played a game called beauty parlor, where they would confiscate all of their mom's makeup and then take turns rouging each other's cheeks and painting each other's nails their favorite color pink. (Of course I played that game too, but never thought to make a living at it!)

Many years later, college educated and in job-search mode, they began reminiscing about the spa parties they threw for the neighborhood girls. Sweet memories of perfumed creams and glittery eye shadows came wafting back. Then came the proverbial (and eventually

DO-IT-YOURSELF SPA NIGHT

If you're looking for a cheap do-it-yourself spa night, the finest ingredients you can use are already sitting in your kitchen. Who needs expensive creams and state-of-the-art machines? As long as it's just you and your Broad Squad, who cares if the avocado goes into the guacamole or on your face? (I can't say the same for the tortilla chips.)

1. For a cleanser, apply yogurt straight from the refrigerator; let it dry, then splash it off with warm water.

2. For a refreshing lift, try a mask made out of mashed cucumber. Apply, then relax for five minutes.

3. Give your girlfriends an instant facial by applying a mixture of half a mashed

(cont.)

avocado and two egg whites. Let stand until dry, then splash off with water.

4. Add brown sugar to the above, massage in small circles, and voilà, you have a microdermabrasion facial!

5. Place cold tea bags over your eyes to soothe the redness. In case of swelling, try a dab of Preparation H. (I've tried this and it works!)

6. Treat your feet! First, rub heels and soles with a pumice stone. Mix a few drops of peppermint extract with a handful of unscented lotion and you have homemade mint foot cream. No toe licking! (Or if there is, we don't want to know.)

very lucrative) big idea: Why not package those girlie-girl evenings as a party in a box for bachelorette parties, birthdays, or a simple Girls' Night In? That's pretty much what they did, and now, not only are they very lucky sister-friends, they are also very rich!

Chapter Six

Girlfriends and Men

Men \'men\ The single most discussed topic among Broad Squads besides cute shoes and magic bullet diets. Stoked with the right amount of time and wine, a relationship confessional can often lead to a fascinating conversation about sex, no sex, and the universal one-liner: "I'll have what she's having." Accessories: Please refer to *Sex and the City* reruns. Specifically, the Samantha episodes.

BESIDES DIETING AND dealing with our mothers, nothing causes a Broad Squad more exasperation than the men in our lives. The truth is, as much as I love my husband Richard (twenty-five years of marriage, two daughters, two dogs, and one goldfish later), my girlfriends are the ones who understand me more than even he does. My Broad Squad loves me unconditionally, indulging me in large cappuccinos and five-mile hikes whenever I need to exercise (and laugh) my stressed-out life away. Before the women in my Broad Squad were married, collectively we had a respectable share of men travel through the revolving door of our lives. Thankfully, many were Elvises—that is to say, they left the building—and the ones who stayed were by and large good ones. But every step along the way, my girls have been fiercely devoted to one another, always cheering one another on to perform our personal best. And here's the key: always using our conversations to support and preserve our emotional friendships. Long after I've asked my husband, "Are you listening to me?" my girlfriends are still here, noting my every word.

That's why the title of this book, *The Secret Language of Girlfriends*, is major. In order to survive, we have developed a lexicon that allows us to fly beneath the radar of the other gender. We can communicate right under their noses without men having a clue as to what we're saying. It's like buying that frivolous but completely cute pair of shoes and paying cash so it never shows up on the credit card.

Our dialogue is a verbal handbook of endurance, and we deserve credit for keeping each other afloat in life's rough seas. But this need to connect to one another—from the telephone to the beauty parlor—has long been categorized and belittled as "just a girl thing." As it turns out, our secret language (and all that gossip) isn't quite so inconsequential after all. Scientists are finally concluding that women's friendships have played a critical role in human evolution. Men may do important things together, such as go to war or to the office or to a baseball game, but we women hunt and gather, too. Many of the rituals described in this book are not only our way of delivering laughter and comfort to one another, but also a means of increasing our chances of survival. This phenomenon of women taking care of each other is termed *tend and befriend*—meaning the more time we spend together, the healthier we are and the happier our children grow up to be.

Our girlfriend language is universal. Go anywhere in the world and it's the same. After dinner, if a woman says she's tired, her man will think she wants a cup of coffee, when she really means that he better not get his hopes up for later.

These are just two examples of the fact that men just don't get it. They give their opinions when all we want is for them to listen. Men drop news like a ton of bricks, while a girlfriend can make even tragedy seem light as a feather. Some men believe they have all the answers to life on their own—no discussion necessary; women can spend hours analyzing one issue. It continues to amaze me that a guy can go away on a fishing trip and return home totally unaware that his buddy is breaking up with his wife. The only relevant piece of new information they have on their "bud" is the size of his speckled trout.

Some men are incapable of listening to our inflections to determine our real feelings. For example, when we're asked why we're upset and we say we're not upset, men are never able to interpret our monotone as "I'm unbelievably

upset—so upset I'm telling you I'm not upset." But what do
you expect from a gender that puts so little value on com-
munication, even with each other? By contrast, girlfriends
can spend an entire week together in a hotel room and still

YOU SAY	GIRL'S RESPONSE	GUY'S RESPONSE
I pulled an all-nighter.	Let's go for coffee.	No wonder you're such a mess.
I ate a whole carrot cake.	You needed beta-carotene.	No wonder your thighs look bigger.
Do I look fat in this?	Absolutely not.	Pretty much.
How do I call you?	Here's my seventeen numbers.	Pager (he's married).
It's not you, it's me.	It's me.	It's you.

FIVE GIRLS YOU NEED ON YOUR ROMANCE BROAD SQUAD

1. *The Scout.* The gal who leaps ahead in your relationship to research and investigate a guy's intentions before you lose your heart to him.

2. *The Personal Shopper.* The friend who makes sure your guy knows what you want for your birthday (and it's *never* a kitchen appliance).

3. *The Best Actress Nominee.* She's the one who will make sure you accidentally bump into that guy you wanted to meet. Her acting ability is atrocious, but he's either too unsuspecting or clueless to notice.

4. *The Call Girl.* The friend who will drop everything to accompany you to a party,

call each other as soon as they get in the door at home.

The great thing about girlfriends is that if we're going through a hard time, we don't angrily grab our golf clubs and slam the door behind us. We don't turn on ESPN at full volume to drown you out, and we tend not to cover our entire face with a newspaper spreadsheet. Instead, we hang in for the bad times, empathizing with each other rather than leaving at the first sign of trouble.

That's why we can obsess about our sex lives, weight, hair products, kids, and jobs without judgment. We can shop, cook, eat, drink, and laugh, making life easier for one another in the process. In fact, when times are bad and we lose ourselves, our girlfriends know where to find us. Friendships are the one place we are vulnerable, and we can tell our best friends secrets we wouldn't even tell our therapist. Our secret language is a kind of grown-up blood pact, and violating this trust is unspeakable and punishable by removal of all friendship privileges. Any girl knows that.

(cont.)

knowing she will be abandoned the moment you connect with a certain guy. The trick here is that next weekend, you'll do the same for her.

5. *The Revenge Girl.* If you've been dumped, she'll be your 911 emergency rescue friend. She also knows how to disconnect his car wiring and gently release his emergency brake while his car is parked on a hill.

Married Girlfriends

Every three seconds, somewhere in the world a woman grumbles, "Men!" as she tries to explain to her husband how to use the microwave for the umpteenth time. No one told us we would be in for years of men flicking through channels, never asking for directions, and always leaving the toilet seat up. Someone should have published *The Rules for Marriage* and handed it out to each of us on our wedding day. It would include all those little laws you wouldn't suspect. For example, the rule about plumbers. When the toilet backs up, contrary to your instincts, you should not call the plumber; instead, you must call your husband first to see if *he* wants to fix it. If he says yes, you must accompany him to the hardware store, follow him around as he drools over all the toys he would love to buy (but would never use), and then in the end, call the plumber anyway. And men think *we're* complicated?

Relationships are frustrating because as women we are natural multitaskers, able to cook dinner and assemble Lego airplanes while teleconferencing and answering e-mail at the same time. We problem-solve even while sleeping, often waking up knowing the answer to the most puzzling problems, such as whether you wear gold or silver with your winter whites. We assume that men can do the same, which is sadly untrue.

We get into trouble dealing with stress—theirs and ours. There's a reason women live longer than men. Rather than work out his troubles, a man will turn on the television and lose himself. We women want to talk out our troubles, but usually our husbands/boyfriends are unavailable, either watching TV or reading the paper. (Never both.) That's why we rely on our girlfriends and the secret language we share.

My Richard

It's truly unfair that we can't have an alteration shop for our husbands, the same way we take our pants in to be fixed. But love them or leave them, there's no changing them.

Recently I was having trouble finding a new sofa that my husband liked as much as I did. My friend Cathie suggested that it might be easier to find a new husband, but I'm still looking for that "completely harmonious sofa." I'm keeping the husband.

Do you think our husbands realize that many of the "secret

SECRET LANGUAGE LEXICON

Fine Used to denote a woman's exasperation in an argument with her "better half" (their term, not ours). The word is generally used at the end of a prolonged "discussion" where the woman knows she's right and is tired of trying to convince him otherwise.

Whatever See *fine*.

Nothing's Wrong Everything is wrong.

We Need to Talk You are up a creek. Wait for *fine* or *whatever* to signal that the argument is over.

We Need to Talk! Either she's pregnant or she just won the lottery.

I Love that Movie A witty, selfless leading lady will

(cont.)

end up on the top of the Empire State Building with a kind widower and his cute little boy. No car bombs, high-speed chases, or bank robberies involved.

I love you Put a lid on it! She wants love, not sex.

language" conversations we've been having all these years have been about them? I'm sure Richard, for one, would be appalled if he knew what I was discussing with my girlfriends in the kitchen while he and the guys TiVo the replays in the family room. His snoring, his driving, his repetitive jokes (you could set your watch at a party by which joke he's telling), having to explain—again—exactly where the Mini-Vac is located. The latter despite the fact that he himself installed it and is standing right next to it as he asks "where?"

Richard, God bless him, is as oblivious to our secret girlfriend language as most of the men I know. He takes everything at face value. Even when I'm clearly upset, if I tell him nothing is wrong he's more than willing to accept that everything's fine. With consistent and impeccably bad timing, he chooses the low end of our daughter's teenage mood swings to take a pressing interest in her life, doggedly investigating her crankiness. Where I might offer her some comfort in hot chocolate or a new mango-and-vanilla body wash, Richard undertakes a military-style interrogation. Has she fought with a friend at school? Stressed over an upcoming exam? Does she want to take a ride to the hardware store with him? That's when she shoots her father a look that says, "Yeah, Dad. That's perfect. I really want to walk up and down the aisles comparing nuts and bolts." As she bursts into tears and flees the room, he looks as if we're crazy or speaking another language. Which, if he must know, we are.

Losing a Girlfriend to a Guy

As strong as our ties are to each other, there's always that phase we go through when one member of our Broad Squad catches the

---

THINGS A GOOD FRIEND WILL TELL YOU ABOUT YOUR BOYFRIEND

* *If he's too well groomed* He's metrosexual (nice lifestyle, but short on passion—better to find a manly man).

* *If he exercises too much* He's eventually going to look better than you (drop him).

* *If he's too neat*   He may be a touch obsessive and moving into metrosexual land (see first point).

* *If he is too affectionate* You may like it at first, but too late you'll realize he's a stalker (get out while you still can).

dreaded romance disease. Suddenly this perfectly logical, sensible gal turns into someone we barely recognize. Like deprogrammers, the rest of us have to go in and reclaim her. We've all witnessed girlfriends with brains the size of Hummers plummet to all-time lows while under the influence of a man. Your friend who never had time for cooking is suddenly whipping up her man's favorite gourmet meals from scratch. Your friend who always knew everything about everything hasn't read a newspaper in weeks and hasn't a clue about what's happening in the world. (Worse still, she doesn't care.) But inevitably, reality sets in. Prince Charming pulls a disappearing act, and your hopelessly devoted friend is crushed. She cries, refuses to answer her phone, and takes time off from work. Of course when the tears and the tranquilizers begin, it's time to call in the Broad Squad. We're the ones who run in when she discovers her knight in shining armor isn't as great as she thought. But we could have told her that.

In fact, a recent study shows that our Broad Squads are more accurate predictors of whether our relationships are going to work than our boyfriends, the late-night love psychic, or even our mothers. According to Dr. Stephen Drigotas,

---

Celebrity Secret

Single girls are no longer waiting for Prince Charming to pop the question to show off that diamond ring. Actresses like Cameron Diaz, Halle Berry, and Sharon Stone are sporting bling-bling on their right hands. Promise rings allow us to show off our own achievements and to celebrate with girlfriends who are proud of us.

Ph.D., a professor of psychology at Southern Methodist University, girlfriends have been proven to be clairvoyant. As it turns out, not only do we talk to each other about our love lives, but we give out extra bits of information that turn our gal pals into walking encyclopedias on the subject of romance. Our secret language not only allows us to listen to our friend's words but gives us an intuitive understanding of how close she is to the edge. For example, if she's kind of dreamy, with a glint in her eye and a glowing complexion, we know she's in the zone. We can let her be for a while. But if she's sitting bolt upright, a strained and constant smile on her face

THE GIRLFRIEND RULES OF ROMANCE

1. You must listen to your girlfriend obsess over every little detail of her new Mr. Right, including the name of his dog and his you-know-what.

2. No dating each other's exes. Once he's been tried, you must be true.

3. Don't criticize her man, even after it seems they've broken up. If they get back together, you'll pay the price. So support her when she complains, but don't lay into him until you're sure the relationship is dead. And not Glenn-Close-in-the-*Fatal-Attraction*-bathtub-scene dead; I mean *dead* dead.

4. Here is the eleventh commandment: Never put boys

while she tries to convince you how happy she is in her new relationship, we know she's unglued—ready for a 911 girlfriend intervention. So while our girlfriend is blinded by infatuation, her Broad Squad knows she's too dazzled to notice he doesn't call when he says he's going to . . . or that his "natural hair" looks suspiciously like a toupee. It's our job to point out that not only is he not her type, but that we are scientifically proven to be the best love meter of anyone she knows—including her therapist.

Single Again

When we first embark on that agonizing stage in life known as being Single Again, girlfriends rank right below ice cream in terms of survival requirements. Not only do we give each other love, reassurance, and support, we are each other's lifelines to our saner selves, living proof there was once a time on Planet Earth when we were absolutely dignified and didn't need Kleenex for our constant tears.

(cont.)

before girls. Girls come first in the girlfriend code.

5. After a breakup, no matter how cool the guy may have been, if he has rejected your friend, he's officially dirt. After all, there's got to be something wrong with him, because you know she's the greatest girl who ever lived.

There is a secret language we all speak when a girlfriend enters (or reenters) that new phase of being Single Again. The post-breakup girlfriend bonding stage is just the beginning of the emergency Broad Squad patrol. After all, only a girlfriend would listen to you whine that nobody will ever love you again without once rolling her eyes. She will call you more faithfully on Valentine's Day than any man ever will, and she's right there with you when your symbolic new couch arrives at your symbolic new apartment. She'll mail you sweet and funny cards, scanning the shelves to find just the right message and tone.

THE BOYFRIEND BOX

If you want a man who wants to make you the center of his universe without a fight in sight, then a Boyfriend-in-a-Box may be for you. Cathy Hamilton, a happily married mom from Lawrence, Kansas, came up with the concept for a pre-packaged relationship after listening to her single and divorced friends talk about the horrors of serial dating.

Each box is graced with a smiling photo of several new beaus for you to choose from. Each has his own distinct profile and comes with a guarantee that he'll call when he says he will, respect your friends, be sensitive to your moods, and be willing to commit (to you, not to an institution). An ability to separate colored laundry from whites and bring you breakfast in bed is a must. The kit includes a smiling five-by-seven plus a wallet-sized

And she'll hand-deliver vast portions of macaroni and cheese (with a side of protein and a vegetable) to make sure you're eating well.

In order to distract you, she shows up at your door on Saturday morning just to take you to the flea market where the shopping is cheaper (and more varied) than, let's say, Neiman's. To top off a week of pain, your girlfriend will throw you a pizza and margarita party and allow you to trash your boyfriend all night. And of course she'll later get on the phone to have that déjà vu conversation all over again.

Our calls and e-mails are a vital part of her therapy, and our gestures, though sometimes time-consuming, are never forgotten. Any offering is significant. And don't worry too much: According to a recent poll in *Jane* magazine, 86% of female respondents preferred to fantasize about chocolate more than a partner—so she may just need a bag of M&M's. If the chocolate doesn't work, I can personally vouch for late-night television. Hanging out with her until she falls asleep is one of the most generous gifts you can give a girlfriend in need. And I know you know exactly what I mean.

(cont.)

photo and message slips reminding you that he called while you were out and that his flowers had to be redelivered.

Apparently, you don't have to be single to enjoy a Boyfriend-in-a-Box. Hamilton herself says her husband doesn't mind that her personal favorite of the boyfriends, Firefighter Frank, lives with them. Since she has a propensity for kitchen fires, Frank comes in very handy. Hamilton says that married women want and need boyfriends just as much as single women do, and that faking it with a faux lover is the way to go. If firemen aren't your type, there are plenty to choose from. My favorite? Self-Made Stan, a cross between Phil Donahue and Bob Barker. Come on *down*!

Chapter Seven
Holidays and Celebrations

Holidays \'hä-lə-,dāz\ That joyous time of peace and love in which we are nevertheless prepared to kill someone for that last toy or last pair of size 7 leather gloves. Also a legitimate reason to shop till you drop, gain five pounds, and strategize Mistletoe Kamikaze Missions. Accessories: eggnog, spiked punch, Santa hats, and photos you can later use for blackmail. Smile! (Or not.)

HOLIDAYS ARE STRESSFUL enough on their own. I've yet to reconcile the combination of skinny holiday outfits with whipped cream desserts, and the additional family dramas (which could rival any reality show) make a sudden business trip to Kazakhstan an attractive alternative. Holidays are also when we overeat and overspend—in an over-the-top, last-minute impulsive psychotic spree. We need someone to get hold of us, and that someone is usually a Broad Squad loyalist.

Lynn is my holiday gal pal, the girlfriend who cheers up all my family celebration dinners with her great wit and sense of style. We usually end up in conversation apart from our men, often on opposite sides of the room. (Not that they ever notice.) During one of our holiday dinners, I unexpectedly went into labor with my younger daughter, AJ. Never having had children herself, Lynn was totally panicked, almost forgetting how to drive. The trip to the hospital—Lynn at the wheel, me in labor, our two husbands of course giving her conflicting directions—was a skit right out of *Saturday Night Live*. For her heroics and as my honorary holiday girlfriend, I asked Lynn to be AJ's godmother. While I thought this a nice touch, it was also a ploy on my part to ensure that she would have a permanent place at my holiday table. Although, truth be told, I'll never ask her to drive me anywhere again.

Holidays can undoubtedly be stressful when you're married with kids, but when you're single, the potential for unmitigated disaster is large. Of course you can always disappear completely, but reality dictates you and your Broad Squad figure out a way to get each other through the holi-daze with your dignity, alcohol level, and checkbook intact.

When I moved to northern California, many miles away from my family in northern Minnesota, I decided to create new traditions to make up for no snow and no family. Designating my girlfriends as my

KAREN'S BROAD SQUAD TIPS TO GET THROUGH THE HOLI-DAZE

* *Buddy Up!* Take a member of your Broad Squad to holiday dinner parties to rescue you from the lame single guy the hostess invariably seats next to you. One of you can beg off, claiming a prior engagement or— depending on how inspired you feel and how quickly you need to escape—an emergency appendectomy.

* *Bring a Friend Home.* If you're visiting your family, bring home a girlfriend so all your crazy relatives are forced to be on their best behavior. A member of your Broad Squad will deflect their

(cont.)

never-ending curiosity about when you're finally going to get married (or remarried) and whether you're ever going to give them grandchildren (not necessarily in that order).

* *Mall-A-Kid.* If the holiday season gets your biological clock ticking like a time bomb, try this antidote. Take one trip to the mall (preferably the day before Christmas) with your girlfriend's angelic tot and watch him melt down into *The Omen* before your very eyes. A surefire clock-stopper.

* *Do Not Call Your Ex.* According to girlfriend law, we need to stop each other from idealizing our

new extended family, I included them in all my holiday fanfare. I admit, some of my ideas were hit-or-miss. One year my Broad Squad and I tried driving to a tree farm to cut down our very own tree, a tradition that lasted about a second and a half.

But Skip Day is a Karen Neuburger Christmas tradition that's lasted for the past twenty-five years. It begins with kidnapping my two children from wherever they're responsibly supposed to be, then pulling my holiday gal pal Lynn out of work. From there we just, well . . . skip. We buy holiday corsages of pinecones, red roses, and satin ribbons to pin on our wool coats and drive around town gawking at the holiday lights. And of course we wander through stores, where each of us loudly hints (think, "Oh, my God, look at that scarf!") when we find the gift we hope will be waiting for us under the tree. Some girlie-girl time at the cosmetic counter is always a Skip Day essential, right before we get in line to take our picture with Santa—the sorry bunch of us falling out of his lap.

These days all of my holidays include a mix of girlfriends and family, a group that knows how to laugh even as we clean up the post-nosh mess. Every year we retaste the leftovers—why let them go to waste?—while we try (unsuccessfully) to cram everything into the dishwasher. In the end we do the dishes by hand because there's never enough room in the washer. Besides, doing it the old-fashioned way gives

(cont.)

exes. During the holidays, this means preventing the kind of peppermint-schnapps-fueled drink-and-dials that start, "Remember what we did last Christmas Eve?" Loneliness breeds senti-mentality, and exes are all official Ghosts of Holiday Past.

* *Chick Flick.* Take time off the couples circuit and watch a favorite funny movie with your gal pal. Warning: Christmas Eve is no time to watch *Sleepless in Seattle* (the wife is dead, the girlfriend's blonde) or any movie that ends on top of the Empire State Building.

(cont.)

* *Do Not Spend New Year's Eve Alone.* Instead, grab a friend and take a chick trip. Share a hot ski instructor (even if you don't ski and never will). Throw a "single girls only" slumber party, or splurge on a great dinner with a fabulous bottle of vino. Ring in the New Year toasting each other, not Dick Clark.

us more time to gab and postmortem the party.

Shop Till You Drop

I don't mean to sound callous, but one of the key parts of the holidays (well, any that are worth celebrating) is gifts—both giving and receiving them. And gifts in girlfriend language translates to shop till you drop, inhale a latte, and shop some more. Shopping is an activity where Broad Squads thrive; it's a fun, life-affirming, endorphin-producing, quintessential girlfriend experience. That's why they call it retail therapy.

What women innately appreciate, which men will genetically never understand, is that we leave the womb wanting comfortable shoes and a mall. Yes, for us, shopping is a biological imperative! We love the chase: the ecstasy of the pursuit, not to mention the thrill of exposing our credit cards in our favorite department stores. From very early on, we view shopping as an adventure, a form of escape, and a kind of entertainment—a secret language we share together.

Men don't shop; they cross brown loafers off their to-do lists. They look for a specific thing (let's take a wild guess and say a pair of golf pants), and if they can't find it, they leave. It never occurs to them to use their peripheral vision to notice the nearby cashmeres. If a guy needs a shirt, he blindly goes to the shirt rack, selects one, pays for it (answering his cell phone at the checkout), and walks out of the store. Of course we buy the shirt too, but then we go searching for the perfect handbag and shoes to go with it.

Now, all bets are off when it comes to shopping for power tools. Then men hang out for hours pushing buttons and listening to the whir of the drills. The same goes for gadgets. Men will go into electronics stores just to peruse the same television models they saw last week (and of course to catch part of the game). They don't get the thrill that runs through us when we hear "now showing fall!" They don't understand the shock of hearing about this season's hemlines or the urgent need to know whether this year's thick belts will go through the thin loops on last year's pants.

CONFIDENTIALLY YOURS . . .

Leah from Potomac knows firsthand that shopping is the cure-all. She says that the day her first husband left her for another woman, her friends took her downtown to look at bridal dresses, to get ready for wedding number two. Her friends got her up and out to the stores without missing a beat. When she's depressed she says, "I never have shopper's remorse. I only feel bad for the things I didn't buy."

Need is obviously a factor in holiday shopping, but it's all about the fantasy, too. Even though Christmas may seem like an exhausting carousel of department stores and gift wrapping, think of the alternative: Would you really want to live in a world without cargo pants and this season's version of the pashmina?

Holiday Lunch

Last year I was tapped by a Broad Squad who had been faithfully getting together for a holiday lunch for more than a decade. As a newcomer to this group of bright, funny, supportive, lively women, I was touched by the warmth of their welcome (not to mention the mimosas, which flowed abundantly around the table). With everyone's hectic schedules, their celebration is both about getting together to share holi-daze horror stories and about having one last hurrah before the New Year. And the girls move heaven and mirth to be there. Cathie had just had foot surgery, but she insisted on making it to her Broad Squad's annual tradition (her best and most fun seasonal obligation). Mary, who always shows up late, swept into the restaurant wearing a fab coat and bearing brightly wrapped chocolates for all of us. We relaxed and yakked for three hours—great gab, great wine, and great food, all eaten off each other's plates.

Cookie Broad Squad

I love to hear the stories of how different Broad Squads celebrate the holidays. Julie Jacks's Broad Squad (which includes Linda, Cindy, and Molly) has baked together at every holiday for almost fifteen years. They got their name, the I.S. Cookie Bakeoff, from the *Saturday Night Live* skit in which Jane

Curtin is repeatedly called "Jane, you ignorant slut." Their group name pretty much sets the tone for the annual get-together, where the four of them compete against each other for top prize in the cookie bakeoff. Julie tries to edge out her competitors each year with an award-winning family recipe called Grandma's Cup of Everything. Cindy promises each year it is she who will claim victory with her phenomenal Mexican Wedding Cookies—delectably prepared with so much powdered sugar that at every tasting session someone winds up in a semicoma. And sweet Molly, who God bless her still does not know the difference between an egg yolk and an egg white, every year manages to put some concoction together. With enough bubbly, no one cares that her dough is completely inedible. She once unfortunately substituted salt for sugar—oh, well!

The I.S. Cookie Bakeoff Girls first got together in Molly's West Coast beach house when all of them were adjusting to the holidays without snow. Thinking that the smell of freshly baked cookies might just put them into the holiday spirit, they unwittingly forged a holiday tradition and a tight-knit Broad Squad from the same dough. Starting early in the morning, they set out the flour, sprinkles, chocolate chips, and the all-important bloody Marys and peppermint schnapps. By the time noon rolls around, they are singing the Hallelujah Chorus from Handel's *Messiah* as the powdered sugar flies around the room—the closest they get to Minnesota snow.

Of course it's not the cookies that keep the I.S. girls together. This holiday Broad Squad is there for one another all year round—through divorce, the death of parents, even the tragic loss of Cindy's infant son. At that sad juncture, they dropped everything, including Julie's high-profile business, to be at Cindy's side. "It's just what you do," Julie says. "My I.S. Bakeoff women are in my corner when I need them. They are my spiritual rocks, the best girlfriends I have ever had." And, may I say, the best cookie makers too!

Christmas Angel Girlfriends

There are times when even a girlfriend you have never met turns out to be your angel in disguise. Christmas almost didn't happen last year for Susan Warren. With her naval husband deployed in the Arabian Sea, this young mom of a little girl just over a year old didn't have the heart to celebrate. "We had no tree, no decorations, and no husband or daddy," she recalls. "I wanted nothing to do with Christmas." But when one of the women on the base invited Susan and her daughter to her place, she decided getting out of the house was probably the right thing to do. The warm friendship she found that day made the holiday bearable. Looking back on that difficult time, Susan feels deep gratitude for her now-close girlfriend who insisted she share Christmas with her family. Since then, Susan has realized that no one can support you like your girlfriends can. She's continued to turn to other women for support and solace when her husband is overseas. As a result, she has found a new Broad Squad she can always count on. A couple of times a week, she meets them to chat, sip coffee, and discuss how fed up they are with the crazy world they live in.

Susan's good friend Kim accompanied her to doctor's appointments and helped her deal with family issues. Now Kim's husband is posted away for a year, and Susan tries to reciprocate. Just as one angelic girlfriend did for her Christmas Day, she invites Kim and her son over to her home, takes her out to a mall, and hopes her kindness helps lift her friend's spirits a little. Says Susan, "Only women can understand what it's like to be alone during the winter with a small baby, having to do everything on your own. I am so grateful to my friends, not only for taking care of me during the holidays, but for caring about me all the days in between."

Easter Bunnies

Easter without my girlfriends would be a nonstarter, just another egg hunting expedition that results in straw baskets and melted chocolate everywhere. While my kids and grandchildren weave carefully through my yard searching for the dyed eggs I made and hid myself, it is my girlfriends who go in for the

A BROAD SQUAD VALENTINE

Who says you have to spend Valentine's Day with a man in order for it to be worth remembering? Lindsay from Vermont spent the "Heart Day" with her two best girlfriends. They were all single and determined to treat themselves to a great time. They began the evening at a mall buying luxurious items—Lauren bought perfume, Sandy bought a red bra, and Lindsay bought herself a silk scarf. Afterwards, they treated themselves to a wonderful dinner at a little French place, where they spent hours talking, drinking wine, and eating. Even today, on Valentine's Day Lindsay still buys herself a silk scarf. And even though she's been married for ten years, she still keeps in touch with the girlfriends who were her first true Valentines.

kill. They're not above throwing aside the kids on their quest for the silver-wrapped first prize. I swear you've never seen an Easter egg hunt until you've seen my holiday gal pal Lynn struggling up the hill in her red stilettos, determined to find the eggs I've buried in the back of my hilly rock garden. While her dedication to fabulous shoes is commendable, it's a little like watching a train wreck as she precariously hops the fence and picks her way over the rocks.

My girlfriend Shelly always generously brings her famous sour cream coffee cake, knowing it's her ticket into the egg hunt. She puts on her game face, laughing and cooing at the kids before suddenly sprinting into action, mowing down whoever is in her way, determined to win first place. Kids step aside as she runs them over, rounding the corner of the house and heading to the finish line (better known as the picnic table).

Gerri, the doctor's wife, who tries to throw everyone off with her demure little sweater set and straw hat to match, transforms into a wild woman during the main event. All the members of my Broad Squad are the show. May the Olympics of egg-hunting bring us all together for many years to come.

CELEBRITY SECRET

Who says Valentine's Day has to be for sweethearts? Why not a celebration of sisterhood? Sharon Sacks, the Los Angeles–based premier social event planner, who has orchestrated parties for Madonna and the Olsen Twins, did just that: hosted a Broad Squad Cupid fest. She asked every guest to bring a dozen of her favorite pink flowers, and then presented a mixed bouquet to each guest as favors. Drinks were raspberry frothy, and desserts of baby pink snowballs and individual strawberry mousses touched every girl's heart.

Girlfriends and Celebrations

Celebration \'se-lə-'brā-shən\ An excuse for Broad Squad lunches and dinners, filled with wonderfully sappy toasts and "meaningful" presents. (Check out the Frederick's of Hollywood wrapping paper!) An opportunity to rejoice, be grateful, and hug every girlfriend for every mile(stone) you have seen each other through.

Fiftieth Birthday

There Ellen was, about to turn fifty, and there seemed to be two options: throw herself off a cliff or throw herself a party. Happily, she chose the latter. In terms of life's big-ticket items—husband, kids, property, bank balance—there might not be much she could claim as her own, but she did realize she was wealthy beyond measure when it came to family and girlfriends. One girlfriend was even generous enough to host the party at her house—and her "house" was three gloriously restored farmhouses in the French countryside. (Not too shabby!) And so, La Fête en France was held in late July 2004.

In addition to Ellen's New York- and California-based family (her mother, two brothers, two sisters, three nieces, a nephew, an aunt, and two cousins . . . and that's barely scratching the surface of the clan), eight girlfriends traveled to France for the event, journeying from Florida, New York, Los Angeles, England, and Spain. Having seen enchanting photographs of her earlier stays in this Provençal paradise, Ellen's girlfriends were eager to visit the place themselves . . . but of course Ellen claims that celebrating her birthday was the only reason they were there. And what a celebration it was!

Between all three houses, she was able to comfortably accommodate everyone. She stayed in the small guest cottage, her family took up the main house, and the third turned into a girls' dorm for the Broad Squad. Every detail of the weekend seemed to fall perfectly into place: from the party favors she'd prepared (cosmetic bags festooned with Parisian designs and filled with "appropriate" items like reading glasses, chewable calcium, eye gel—and an Eiffel Tower key chain) to the well-coordinated arrivals of her guests, who found their way via plane, car, train, and cross-Channel ferry, to the dinner rolls the local baker had personalized with each guest's first name (and which made for perfectly edible place cards!). Even the iffy summer weather cooperated.

After months of careful planning, would Ellen's fantasies and expectations exceed the actual event? Not for a moment. The evening was magical and merveilleux beyond any possible dream; a lovely, luscious outdoor multicourse dinner that began when she welcomed her assembled guests shortly after 8:00 P.M. and carried on until the sinfully rich choco-late birthday cake was brought out at nearly 2:00 A.M.!

She was relieved to see that just a few symbolic candles had been placed on the cake—and delightfully surprised to discover that one of her English friends had brought with her dozens of Fourth of July–type sparklers. Everyone lit theirs in unison as they serenaded her, setting the late-night landscape ablaze with glittering, twinkling lights. But truly, she hardly needed them. She felt lit from within with loving good wishes and will carry the glow from that wondrous evening with her always. And speaking of sparklers, three of the gifts she received contained diamonds . . . so she should probably rethink that earlier statement about life's big-ticket items.

The Reunion

It takes only about a year to get ready for a high school re-union. By the time you buy the dress, lose some weight, buy another dress, gain the weight back, and have nothing to wear—well, that's a year right there. But once you get over your neuroses, a reunion is a time to get silly, bury the hatchet, reminisce with old friends and torment the queen wannabe who stole your high school sweetheart, and now looks sorry she did! (Oooooo! Meow!)

When I went home for my high school reunion, I had a two-part plan. Of course I wanted to huddle with my high school Broad Squad, reliving some of the best and worst years of my life. But I also wanted to have AJ, my youngest daughter, see firsthand the importance of a girlfriend bond that spans decades.

HIGH SCHOOL REUNION

Translation: A chance to gloat in revenge over the kids who tormented you way back when and now have to deal with your success. An opportunity to see through your daughter's eyes how geeky we all dressed and danced in our youth. A reason to diet so they'll never see you sweat . . . or fat.

Accessories: Polaroid camera and a corsage to make up for the one your prom date forgot to bring you.

Even though AJ and I got in late the night we flew into Duluth, we immediately gave a call to Vickie, my absolute number one girlfriend, and told her to meet us at the pizza joint in town. I immediately spotted her green Dodge 4 by 4 truck, which as a teenager, she drove in the powder puff derby stock-car races at the fairgrounds. Vickie was sitting in "our" booth with her back to the door, just the top of her short highlighted hair showing. When we sneaked up on her, there was much shrieking and laughing, and then she and I sat down to our bottles of Michelob Lite (AJ was still too young).

Even though it had been ten years, sitting down with Vickie at the Shamrock with a bottle of beer and the best pizza ever was as natural as slipping into my most comfortable moccasins. We had sat hundreds of times in that very same booth, discussing the mysteries of life: boyfriends, hair color, and the age-old question of how short was too short to trim our cut-off jeans. AJ, listening intently to our gabfest, became very inquisitive, struggling to keep track of her mother's Broad Squad life. "Who was this Mike guy, anyway? What year was the Chevy Impala? How did you and Vickie get that keg of beer?"

The next day it was time to meet the rest of the Broad Squad to decorate the Elks Hall for the reunion. After cleaning out every florist in town of their purple and white (our school colors) flowers, we walked into the hall to find my friend Pauline (aka Up-the-Tree-Pauline, so nicknamed for the night she climbed a tree and stayed up there for two hours to escape the county police trying to break up our beach party).

Even though it had been longer than I would like to admit since I'd seen her, there was no mistaking tall and leggy take-charge Pauline. I was so happy she hadn't changed a bit. Nancy, dressed in capris and an oversize blouse reminiscent of a *Father Knows Best* rerun, looked like she'd stepped right out of our yearbook. Carol, always presidential, taped the class photos on the walls, while Vickie, with her typical need to approve any deviations from her decorating plan, allowed me to fall back into my submissive role without missing a beat.

The thing about high school reunions is that you get to see how far back your Broad Squad really goes. Those relationships of yore were important touchstones for all of us— early lesson plans that gave us the ability to expand our circle of friends as we moved through life.

What makes me happiest about all the holidays and celebrations I've enjoyed with my Broad Squad is that I have made a wise long-term investment in the best blue-chip stock of all: my girlfriends. With every dinner and teary toast,

I look around the table and know no matter what happens in my life, I will always be able to count on these women for comfort, support, and a fabulous birthday party with a discreet number of candles on the cake. I love that we have celebrated so many of our good times together, and that we have created our own rich history. Our shorthand is awesome. We get each other's jokes, fill in each other's blanks, and finish each other's stories in the lexicon of our secret language. Most of all, I love that my friends have become my chosen family. And if you think blood is thicker than a Broad Squad, come by my house some holiday time when we're crying from laughing so hard, and you will see a group of girlfriends who over the years have become my sisters, special women I now thankfully and consciously celebrate every day of the year.

Chapter Eight
Girlfriends and Crafts

Girlfriend Craft Night \\'g ər(-ə)l-,frend 'kräft 'nīt\\ A destressing session with your Broad Squad where you create a handmade scarf or potholder to give your gal pal on her birthday. Warning: Objects may appear less than perfect up close. Get over it. A craft made with love defies perfection!

OKAY, I ADMIT IT: my house is covered with UFOs. Not the unidentified flying object variety, but unfinished objects. Everywhere I look, my unfinished craft projects lie like

CRAFTY LADIES

The Ladies of the Oneonta Craft Club admit to a lot of laughter and gossip but not a lot of crafting during their twenty-five-year girlfriend get-togethers. Most of their energy goes toward catching up with each other and eating dessert. To be fair, at Christmastime last year, they did create some Christmas wreaths. But now their focus is upping their cash flow so they'll be flush for their annual Ladies shopping trip in the New Year. The ten members say their craft club is like therapy—better than a good night's sleep or a day at the spa.

guilty reminders in assorted boxes, closets, and trunks. Half-crocheted afghans, half-embroidered pillows, a set of rusty decoupaged homemade lamps—what was I thinking?—stare back at me from baskets by the kitchen table, in the laundry room, and on shelves in the garage. There among my gardening tools is the aborted family photo project I'll finish one day; right behind it, a millennium-themed ceramic bowl that I may rework for the year 3000. (Did I miss that deadline, or what?)

But I've made peace with my UFOs. The fun is in the journey, not the destination. And so against the wishes of my family (who argue we could buy a new car for what Mom spends on abandoned craft projects), I will continue to devour craft magazines and start projects with the enthusiasm of someone with a severe case of amnesia, a romantic who cannot remember that getting to the finish line is not one of her greatest assets.

I love the optimism I feel when I embark on new craft project, which seems imbued with the promise of new life—minus the dirty diapers and midnight feeds. Going to the craft store to buy my materials makes me feel like a girl again, buying my new school notebooks each year, with fresh white pages and no doodling. I know you are out there too, crafty girlfriends—flying below the radar, painting, glazing, scraping away. I've seen you alone in restaurants, on the beach, and on jury duty. And I've been with you at craft conventions, where thousands of you delight in taking your grandmother's favorite pastimes and fashioning them into creative stress relievers, not to mention quality girlfriend time.

Scrapbooking Mania

You have no idea what chaos looks like until you've seen scrapbooking mania in action. Across the country, at craft goddess gatherings, throngs of women are cutting loose: scissors in hand, covered in decorative glitter as they huddle over photo albums filled with memories. In an environment as noisy as the floor of the New York Stock Exchange, women scream across the long tables for ideas as they design pages commemorating their baby's first haircut, their parents' golden wedding anniversary, or their Broad Squad chick trips.

These are not our grandmother's simple albums. They are extravagant creations: love letters, artwork, and fancy frills added to photos that before this craze sat in dusty boxes in the attic. I have seen scrapbooks jammed with four generations of family mementos, and I have seen one album, wrapped in fancy light blue ribbon, dedicated completely to ultrasound photos. It's impossible to deny that scrapbooking has become an obsession for many.

The Memory Maker Girlfriend Weekend

For years, my customers have been writing to tell me about wearing their KNs to all-night pajama parties at cropping weekends. Cropping weekends? I had to check this out for myself.

Cut to a national hobby and craft show, officially called

Camp Memory Makers. I enter a massive convention center jammed with Broad Squads playing together, all acting like they'd just opened up a new box of sixty-four crayons, bonding over a million samples of printed and colored paper, colored pens, archival boxes, totes, scissors, and glue. I had but one thought before I too dove in: if thousands of us can get this excited about a scrapbook, maybe we all have to get out of the house more! You think?

The Memory Makers' weekend scrapbook fest is the female version of the boys' fishing weekend—minus the beer, belching competitions, and the yucky smell. But just like the fishing weekend, scrapbooking camp is all about the company and the big catch. In our case: the award for the best costume!

Having planned the weekend for months, the Memory Makers have so much pent-up excitement for the event, it's only natural that each group of girlfriends celebrates with its own theme, name, song, and costumes. The Tiki Tatters showed up in their grass skirts and leis, the Pajama Mamas in their custom-made fringe-trimmed PJs, the outrageous Survivor Group looking fresh from some far-off exotic jungle, and the Divas dressed all in pink (what else?), flaunting their hot pink boas and jeweled tiaras. But there was no Miss America—type competition here. These women bonded as tightly as the acid-free glue that held together their scrap book creations.

Of course, such girlish freedom comes at a cost. Julie had convinced her husband that their anniversary fell on a Wednesday, not that Saturday, so she wouldn't have to miss a moment of the festivities—hats off to her for the best cover-up story of the weekend! (And for putting up with a husband who has not a clue.) Terri, who had never been away from her family, had downloaded her kids' pictures onto fabric and sewed their darling faces all over her PJs so she wouldn't forget what they looked like. "Get over it! Just enjoy yourself," I told Terri, who laughed and admitted she'd already forgotten she had a family. After kibitzing with her, I check out the ladies' room, where a steady soundtrack of laughter and squeals accompanied by spurts of loud rock music erupts every time the doors open and close.

Wait! There's More

On Saturday morning the excitement really got going. After a jolt of some caffeine we all rushed off to our classes to learn new techniques for bookmaking, quick scrapping designs, and embellishment essentials. The learning lasted all day for some, while others sneaked off that afternoon to the big mall next door for some of that great girlfriend pastime—retail therapy.

At 8:00 P.M., cropped out and shopped out, we all gathered in the main hall for the Scrappy Awards! Sparing no amount of pink, we re-created the Pink Ladies PJ party from *Grease*, complete with a frilly Olivia Newton-John bed (sadly without John Travolta in it). Big girls, tiny girls, young girls, not-so-young girls—all gave themselves permission to be wild and crazy. Multitasking as only girlfriends can, we dished about men, kids, hair, TV shows, and our bodies while snacking on homemade cookies and playing truth or dare (even though no one needed the dare). After a rousing good-bye chorus of "I Am Woman," the scrappy girls returned home with goody bags filled with Waitress Pink nail

A SCRAPPY BIRTHDAY SURPRISE

Summon your Broad Squad and surprise your birthday gal with a scrapbook devoted to her wonderful life. Invite each member of her girlfriend team (be sure to include her college roommate and hairdresser) to recall their favorite moments, inside jokes, and sexy secrets on a scrapbook page. Then bind them together into a tribute book that will be the best birthday gift she's ever received. Don't forget to include:

* *E-mails. The one she meant to send to you "about last night," but sent to her office instead.*

* *Letters. The one she sent from Paris when she met that gorgeous French guy. Ooh-la-la!*

polish, PJs, and robes. But the winning team, which the judges admitted was incredibly hard to select, all received embellished hairnets, complete with Velcro rollers. And one lucky contestant walked away with a huge—and I mean coffee-can-sized—jar of Dippity-Doo hair gel. I so wanted to win!

Scrap Girls

Before I ventured into Memory Maker land, I enjoyed a scrappy Girls' Night In with my friends Linda, Holly, and Shelly. After September 11, 2001, we all felt the need to distract ourselves and keep busy. So our Monday night get-togethers have evolved into a trendy creative diversion from reality. The obsession with scrapping is so in vogue, Shelly claims there is no such thing as original anymore in scrapbooking. Most of our ideas come from what she calls "scraplifting": girlfriend translation for getting ideas from nature, gardens, and other women.

Scrapbooking, to distinguish it from other obsessions, is the only girlfriend activity where food doesn't actually play a leading role. Dinner is inhaled and then out come the cutters, pens, glue dots, papers, stickers, archival boxes, and non-toxic sprays—all packed in rolling carts. We have taken our Scrapping Nights In on the road, branching out on road trips around the Bay Area where we comb scrapbook stores for sister scrappers and new tools. We have definitely developed a

(cont.)

* *Graduation cap tassels.* From the hats you tossed into the air together . . . no worries if you can't remember what happened after that!

* *Ticket stubs.* To the Natalie Merchant concert you scored at the last minute.

* *Boarding passes.* From your first chick trip together.

* *Cocktail napkins.* From the bar you went to when you turned twenty-one and could finally drink (legally, anyway).

* *Fortunes.* From the cookies at your favorite Chinese restaurant.

* *Poetry.* Verse that you know makes her cry.

(cont.)

* *Valentine's Day cards.* Give her the one she sent to you the year no one else thought to.

* *One lock of purple hair.* From the worst dye job ever!

Paste on the glitter, and pour on the glue pens and dried flowers. Just add wine and laughter!

P.S. The book works for reunions, graduation parties, wedding and baby showers too.

secret language with each other. If one of us discovers a great new concept, material, or idea, another of us says, "I concur." That's code for everyone to freeze in our tracks and look.

We've taken chick trips to Bodega Bay on a Weekend Crop: translation, a weekend of napping, chick flicks, and crop feed (mashed potatoes, turkey with gravy, or deep-fried tacos with tons of toppings). In the time we have been together, my scrapbook is still a UFO. But Shelley created a beautiful book for her son for his high school graduation, and Linda captured her recent trip to France with colors and textures inspired by Provence. Even if I never finish, I love our time together. I just need to find a place in my garage where my scrapbook can go AWOL for a while without my husband noticing!

Take Back the Knit

"Crafting," pronounces Debbie Stoller, the author of *Stitch 'N Bitch*, "is the new rock and roll, baby. We are taking back the knit." She is so right. Knitting has become way cool: a viable activity for hip urban Broad Squads and stressed-out suburbanites, all of whom find crafting a way better escape than Prozac. Everywhere, trendy goddesses, or as Debbie calls them, "righteous chicks with sticks," are knitting like Grandma—without the rolled-up stockings. Stylish girlfriends that we are, we've thrown out the so-last-generation tea cozies to make way for punk-rock handbags and cell phone holders made from materials such as mohair, angora, even vegan

---

THE SECRET LANGUAGE OF THE CRAFTY GIRLS

Craft of the Month Girl
The girl who flits from knitting to quilting to scrapbooking without ever finishing one project. An example would be me.

Embellishment Queen
The girl who manages to outschmaltz everyone with nostalgic memories.

Craft Roadkill A project that went wrong and ended up hidden in the back of the closet.

Closet Crafter The girl who doesn't let anyone else in on her ideas. Sooo not cool!

The Craft Diet Using your hands to craft instead of eat.

(cont.)

Craft Lifting   Stealing someone else's ideas (the Closet Crafter's worst nightmare).

Handmade Lite   Buying most of the craft prefab at a store and adding a small embellishment, like changing the buttons on a store-bought sweater.

Hell on Wheels   The girl who is knitting so fast, she could injure you with her sticks.

fox (translation: fake fur, no dairy). The list of funky patterns is endless. Try a skull-and-crossbones sweater or a Wonder Woman bikini, even a knitted bridesmaid blouse. If your girlfriend is preggers, there's even a pattern for an heirloom-quality baby blanket with a matching hat.

An added plus? Knitting gets you recognized. One of the members of a knitting group called Purl and Hurl raves about how she loves the attention their handicrafts draw and the wow factor handicrafts generate.

The Lion and the Lamb

If pink is the new black, then knitting is the new yoga. "You have no idea," says Leslie, owner of Manhattan's The Lion and the Lamb. In her best New York accent she declares, "The conversations you hear in this store are better than *The View*." She's right. Enter into her colorful haven of yarn and

CONFIDENTIALLY YOURS . . .

Debbie Stoller, the queen of Stitch 'N Bitch, tells us her group meets in an East Village café where the best seats are the couches right in the window. People always stop to look in and watch the knitters. Says Debbie, "Some of them look like we may as well be churning butter—they think a group of young women knitting is so weird. But the older ladies know. They give us a big thumbs-up!"

thread and you immediately feel like grabbing a pair of sticks to join the fifteen women already seated at one of the long tables in the store, needles flying. Naturally protective of her own Broad Squad, Leslie claims she has met some of the warmest, hippest, most supportive women of her life in her own store. And she knows firsthand how important girlfriends can be. After a twenty-year marriage, Leslie went through a bad divorce last year. Frequently she came into the store crying and was blown away by how compassionate her clientele turned out to be. Never having had a group of girlfriends, Leslie didn't realize how cool other women were until they saw her through her crisis.

Women here share stories about their kids, jobs, pets, men, even accessories. One woman loved another woman's pocketbook so much, she picked up the phone and ordered one that minute and had it hand-delivered . . . right to the knitting table. In fact, many women who have met at the Stitch 'N Bitch sessions later arrange to hook up for drinks or lunch or plan to return to the store at the same time so they can continue their gabfest.

Leslie tells me it's hip to knit. "People used it think it was so grandma, but I've been stitching my whole life," she says. "It's my yoga. It's my therapy. People used to make so much fun of me, but now it's cool. Since ninety percent of knitting is math, mothers who come into the store say their daughters' math skills are zooming, not to mention their fine motor ability."

Knitting and needlework provide a real sense of accomplishment. When you get in the zone, you forget your troubles. Leslie finds that women's inhibitions evaporate when

---

Celebrity Secret

Girlfriends ready for a break will find knitting is a perfect escape. Oscar winner Julia Roberts has her yarn and needles with her on the set for those times between takes. Ditto for supermodel Naomi Campbell between photography shots. Both women agree knitting relaxes them and gives them something to do while they're waiting.

---

they're knitting together. Everyone really opens up because they feel safe, as if they're home. The Lion and the Lamb is a very informal setting so you can sit, do your crafts, nosh or drink coffee or wine.

Says Leslie, "Women of all ages and types come in and liven up the joint. We have nothing in common, but we have everything in common. Then again, that's true of women always. But you know what I say? 'If it's good enough for Julia Roberts, then why not us, too?'"

Quilting

Quilting, unlike scrapping and knitting, has not become the trendy rage of the tragically hip—maybe because it's an art form rooted in so much tradition. It's an emotional piece of business, a handmade quilt, and I am glad our quilters are finally being recognized as the artists they are. I cried like a baby when I first saw the AIDS Memorial Quilt, that beautiful piece of patchwork covered with tender memories of those we have lost. And I have smiled while sewing tiny pieces of fabric with hearts, ducks, and good wishes into a nine-block blanket for a neighbor's baby.

A girlfriend of mine was hanging by an emotional thread following her divorce. She insists she literally kept herself stitched together by creating and quilting something new every week. Time passed as she fashioned her life out of scraps of cloth, and one day she noticed her choice of colors was brighter. She was healing. When she was fully through her blahs, she decided to create a sensual quilt out of white satin and black lace, which is when I knew she was ready to join the dating game once again.

Twisted Sisters

Quilting groups have traditionally been a way to social-ize, a way to meet with other women by literally joining a friendship circle in your church or community center. Nothing has changed in that respect. Women are still getting together every day to stitch their squares, and to make friends as they do. But the artistry of quilting has changed enormously since the days of the quilting bees.

The quilting work of Julie John Upshaw from Dallas, Texas, is displayed in exclusive galleries and art museums throughout the country. Privately, her work commands up to six thousand dollars a quilt. As an art quilter, Julie is part of an elite group who make up only 5 percent of the entire quilting population in the country. Feeling isolated in her specialized art form, she joined a quilter's guild friendship group of about twenty women, eight of whom are the core

CONFIDENTIALLY YOURS ...

Here's what a power-punch combo of good friends and crafts can be: Nineteen-year-old Jessica Porter from Hudson, Florida, and her friend Ruth Ann Pleus decided to use crafts for healing. Together they launched Operation Homefront Quilts, a project to offer comfort to families who have lost loved ones in the war in Iraq. Always patriotic in theme, each quilt takes the girls fifteen hours to make. The families who have received their quilts appreciate their creativity and the memories they preserve.

group. As soon as she met them she knew she had found sisters for life.

Calling themselves the Twisted Stitchers, they meet every week to gossip and work on their individual projects. Besides now having a web page where they communicate daily about their craft, in true girlfriend style they also keep one another current about their daily lives. Each year they take a field trip to the International Quilt Festival, which Julie calls the biggest slumber party in the world: 52,000 women pouring out of buses and hotel rooms, all connected through quilting.

Recently, the Twisted Stitchers decided to work on a quilt together. Julie says it was hard to work on a group project since they had been so used to working on their own. But the round robin approach and group bonding has made all of the challenges worth it. As they sew, patch, and cut, they have gotten closer. There are cancer survivors, women who are going through divorce or the death of a parent, but as Julie says, "We keep each other together . . . just like our quilt. And we push each other's boundaries as we push the definition of quilting further. As we learn about one another, we create our own story both inside and outside the quilting circle."

Chapter Nine

Passing It On: Nurturing the Next Generation of Girlfriends

NONE OF US would be the same without our Broad Squads. When some nameless guy has flown the coop, it is our girl-friends who stand by us, stand up for us, and never stand us up. Although we don't like to admit it, some of us are at that certain age, and a new generation of women stands behind us, ready to come into its own. It's our mission, should we choose to accept it, to pass on the legacy of girlfriendship to our daughters. Through example, we must teach them how important it is to hold on to their girlfriends for dear life, even when life takes them in separate directions.

Too bad there's not a prerequisite for life that says in order for girls to pass go, collect our credit cards, and move away from home, we must have our girlfriends by our side. Just as we have to get a driver's license at sixteen (and get carded before we're twenty-one—supposedly), so too should we be required, at least by girlfriend law, to be certified in the art of Girlfriendship. Courses we would need to pass include Pajama Parties 101, Comparative Approaches to Girls' Nights Out, and Chick Trips in American Film and Literature. Before facing life we'd have to get our diplomas in Honesty, Hand-Holding, Hysterical Laughter, and that all-important life lesson Never Keep Henna Dye in Your Hair for Too Long or It Will Go Orange. Alas, our daughters will have to learn all of this for themselves, poor babies. They may not get it yet, but it's their girlfriends who are going to celebrate their birthdays, make tea, be therapists, feed the dog (and kids), and hand out tissues until there are no more tears to cry.

I could not have survived (nor laughed as much) without my California girlfriend posse Karen, Cathie, Mary, Gerri, and Lynn. Both of my girls adore how my Broad Squad brands every occasion with their particular variety of zaniness and just the right touch: the ideal present, a homemade cake, silly conversation, and the expectation that they, faces beaming, will always occupy a second row in the auditorium for every concert, play, and graduation my girls participated in. Let me assure you, showing up for your Broad Squad's children with a small bouquet, a big smile, and a generous heart is a very big deal, and a lifelong lesson in the art of friendship.

Right now my daughter AJ is on a trip with my friend Lynn, her godmother (aka Auntie Mame), who spirited her away to a Mexican resort for her graduation present. I'm a little miffed I wasn't invited, but I have a feeling the two of them are up to some fabulous conspiratorial no good. (Frankly, I'm afraid to ask.) So besides teaching our daughters to be goddesses, to run with the wolves, and to always wear clean underwear just in case they're ever (God forbid) in an accident, it's also important to teach our daughters the need to forge alliances with their own Broad Squads that will last them for a lifetime—and beyond.

The Mini Broad Squad

Tamara from Orlando makes sure her two young daughters, Hannah and Sara, know how important it is to recruit their very own girl posse. Tamara has been joined at the hip with her Broad Squad (Marty, Kelly, and Andrea) since preschool; it's a bond that has taken them through Barbies, boys, and babies. Krazy Glued together, they felt spending every day with one another during school and summertime wasn't enough. Each evening they would talk to each other for several more hours on the phone. Looking back, the girls don't know how they existed without Instant Messaging—or call waiting!

In college (as often happens) the four girls went their separate ways, pledging different sororities or not pledging at all. Some returned home for the summer, some stayed at school. But like true girlfriends, the quartet always knew (still know) that if they needed anything—a solution to a problem, great news to share—they always had each other—big-time. Even though they were often geographically separated, the band of four made it a top priority to be bridesmaids in each other's weddings and to meet each other's children within their first few days of life. Tamara explains that a strange thing happens every time they reconnect: it's as if no time at all has passed. There are no ill feelings, no apologies needed (although they're always expressed). Amazingly, they simply pick up where they left off.

Tamara's daughters have gotten to know their mother's Broad Squad so well, they view them as part of the family. Even though they are all geographically separate, the families have spent time together skiing (although it sometimes looks more like sliding). They get together for barbecues and birthdays, always hauling out the old yearbooks and photos to show their children their wild, funny hairstyles. (What were they thinking?)

What's gratifying for Tamara is to see that her daughters are also developing solid friendships. Her daughter Hannah and her best friend Niki—friends for five of their ten years—look like inevitable keepers of the Broad Squad flame. Explains Tamara, "I want my daughters to feel safe, knowing that there are women in their lives who would drop everything for them if they needed them, and would always love the person they were yesterday, as well as the person they are today. I want my daughters and her friends to be proud of each other, cherish each other, and share the importance of that devotion to friendship—deep within their souls."

Dream a Little Dream

If you want your girls to grow up showing the world what they're made of (here's a shocker: it's not sugar and spice), then you must instill in them a belief that as long as they clean up their rooms and come home before curfew, anything they can dream is possible. It's up to you and your Broad Squad to give your daughters a clue that life's dreams can come true. Not the kind where some fraudulent prince puts a glass slipper on their foot and they (poof!) become a princess. I'm talking about the dream where hard work meets up with opportunity and your daughters love what they do. And know enough not to try and do it in high heels, not to mention glass slippers.

One of the great pluses of my Broad Squad is that they're so passionate and diverse in what they do. My girls have grown up watching my friends organize political conventions, fund-raise for charity, cook, write books, snowboard, start businesses, and host television shows. They've witnessed

MINI BROAD SQUAD TALK	MOM'S BROAD TALK
Boys	Men
Saturday Night Sleepover	Sunday morning sleep-in
What will you do tomorrow?	All the things you have to do tomorrow
Rock concert	New CD
Orlando Bloom, Aaron Carter	George Clooney, Bruce Springsteen
Birthday wish to be sixteen	Birthday wish to be sixteen again
A juicy little secret	A secret age-defying juice
Long distance boyfriends	Long distance rates
My crazy family	I am crazed from my family
Stuff	Getting rid of stuff

several of my gal pals reinvent themselves: new careers, new husbands, new babies. They've participated as co-conspirators at several surprise birthday parties, and marched down the aisle as flower girls at more than one second marriage. And they've seen struggles within the squad. They've hidden behind closed doors listening to girlfriend spats, major and minor, and then observed how we worked them through. They've seen girlfriends in action and know firsthand how committed we are to one another.

One of the most important lessons we pass on to our daughters is how absolutely important it is to take care of ourselves. Having it all means doing it all, but that martyr routine is so last generation. Girlfriends, if we don't take care of ourselves and each other, then how are we going to keep caring for everyone else? Who is going to drive the car pool? Put dinner on the table? Make the money that pays for dinner on the table (not to mention for the table itself!)? You know the drill, and you've known it for years. It's part of our secret language that we covertly understand that all of us are overscheduled with everyone else's to-do lists. But it's time to put our needs on our own agendas.

Mom Camp

That's why I was thrilled to hear about Mom Camp, the brainchild of Teresa Fudenberg and Mary Kay Bunde-Duchene, who own the umbrella company Wonderful U (as in university). Since college, these two girlfriends have called themselves the FTP Sisters (that's For The People). They had vowed to one day work for the people and not for some insensitive evil boss.

Mom Camp is an opportunity for mothers and daughters to go away together. It shows the younger generation how lifesaving it is for moms to have time out from real life, and time together with their Broad Squads. Besides the giggly fun of being at camp (and of course, the melt-in-your-mouth s'mores), there are exercises to help moms and daughters empathize with one another's realities.

A friend of mine and her teenage daughter attended a workshop in which they were instructed to write down everything they accomplished in a typical day. The daughter wrote down things like talk on the phone with friends, finish homework, write e-mail to hottie new boy, attend volleyball practice, and that great catchall "whatever." (Whatever that

---

CONFIDENTIALLY YOURS . . .

To show how important it is for girls to look after themselves and destress, the American Girl dolls now have their very own spa. Millions of girls aged three to twelve who collect these dolls can pamper them with spa accessories like facial chairs, plush robes, and slippers and the popular spa treatment kit, which includes a terry mitt, facial mask, cucumber slices, pretend nail polish, tiny flip-flops, and toenail decals. At New York City's new American Girl Place, dolls can have their tresses professionally styled at the popular doll hair salon. Wait! I want a day at the spa for me!

---

means.) Mom listed chores like fix breakfast and dinner (and sometimes lunch), check homework, grocery-shop, pay bills, attend kids' sporting events, clean the house, fold laundry, wash car, chauffeur kids to school, and make deadlines at the office. Hello? The result was that her daughter was amazed at how self-centered her own paltry list seemed, and was blown away by realizing how many things her mom did for the

CONFIDENTIALLY YOURS . . .

These days indulging in foot massages and aromatherapy can earn junior Girl Scouts a merit badge. The Stress Less badge is designed to help girls cope with pressure-cooker demands of modern life. Parents and child psychologists are applauding it, saying it complements other attempts to help girls handle stress at younger ages.

family every single day. And here's when the light snapped on: Mom realized how little she was doing for herself and how self-destructive that was in the long run.

After staring at the inequity on paper, the daughters were happy to see their moms spend three days rejuvenating, making new friends, reflecting, taking a deep breath, and relaxing. And the girls promised they would continue to support their moms having some downtime at home (as long as it didn't interfere with the chauffeuring schedule, of course).

As for the cofounders of Mom Camp, like any successful

Broad Squad, the FTP Sisterhood has remained intact. When one of them calls or e-mails the other with the message "FTP!", this doesn't mean next weekend or in a few days. This is secret language for "I need sisterhood *now!*"

Tea at the Ritz

Ever since our "little friend" arrived on the scene and we were rewarded with a book that made no sense and a sanitary pad, we vowed that when it was our turn to tell our daughters about their entrance into womanhood, we would transform the curse into a celebration. Susan was one woman who decided she wanted to create a new tradition in her family, and pass along to her daughter the beauty and joy of this occasion (along with the sanitary pad).

Celebrating your daughters' milestones with your girlfriends and hers is an important element of passing on the Broad Squad customs. Susan and Barbara met when their daughters were in elementary school. They discovered that their sensibilities were similar in many ways, including their attitudes about child rearing, and particularly their ideas about raising daughters. But their friendship wasn't just about their daughters, and almost from the start, there was a connection between them that grew over the years.

When Susan's daughter got her period, Susan wanted to create a positive ritual around it, an event that was celebratory and had a distinctly feminine ring to it. She thought a high tea would be just the thing. It had the necessary pomp and circumstance, some sly humor, and watercress finger sandwiches, too! When she told her girlfriend Barbara about the idea, she shared Susan's enthusiasm. After all, her daughter would experience the same thing one day soon; why not create a meaningful tradition? It would teach their daughters about the female rites of passage and the importance of having the support of close friends.

So there they were at the Ritz-Carlton, Susan and Barbara with their highfalutin expectations of sharing profound words of wisdom (and scones with clotted cream) about this exciting entry into womanhood. But naturally, all the girls wanted to do was inhale the little tea sandwiches and chocolate cakes, and run outside in their best clothes to look at the pretty boats docked by the restaurant. The significance of the moment seemed lost on the girls—but that was fine with their moms. They were successful in re-creating history, building and sharing a special moment that one day would register with their girls. And they were confident that when this moment came for their granddaughters, it would come with the tradition of scones and fancy fixings.

Book Club

In order to get time with your girlfriends (and your daughters) you may want to form a mother-daughter book club, where moms and daughters get together to talk about a piece of fiction and end up discussing their real lives (not to mention indulging in homemade goodies afterwards).

This was certainly the case for Dr. Susan Hasazi of Burlington, Vermont. Susan not only craved more girlfriend bonding time, but desired an opportunity to relate to her daughter Sarah in a relaxed and intimate setting. Cleverly combining the two, she created a mother-daughter book club that is still going strong after eight years. The club has met night after night to discuss books in depth, becoming a very tight-knit group in the process.

Each month, one of the mother-daughter teams chooses

the book and runs the meeting. When the girls were young, they used games to facilitate discussions; now everyone's just down and dirty with outspoken opinions. Meetings are well attended and rarely missed. But the best part of the club is how safe and comfortable Sarah feels with all the other moms, how she knows she could go to any one of them with a problem. Great food, of course, is part of the evening. These girls, young and older alike, discuss, eat, schmooze, and go back to discussing once again.

The great bonus of the group is that Susan and Sarah get to talk about issues that might have never come up at their own kitchen table. Disturbing issues such as date rape, teen pregnancy, and drugs and alcohol have been raised by the girls at the book

FRIENDSHIP TREASURE BOX

Surprise your daughter with a treasure chest that commemorates the value of girlfriends and family in her life. Decorate a beautiful box and fill it with photos of you with your Broad Squad and her Mini Broad Squad. Also, include little mementos of special times you've shared, plus photos from all the trips you've taken together. Include a letter from one of your Broad Squad members telling your daughter how much she loves her. And top it off with birthday and Valentine's Day cards from her friends. Tie the box with a gorgeous silk ribbon and present it to your daughter on her birthday. Make sure all girlfriends (young and old) are there when she opens it.

club, and the group has allowed both mothers and daughters to tackle them head-on.

Girls' Night Out at School

One of the most important values our girls learn from us is how to take care of and respect our bodies. But if you were like me and had trouble walking down the school hallway and chewing gum at the same time, the whole concept of exercise, especially as it related to gym class, was a nightmare.

Enter Noreen, a physical education teacher from Ottawa, Ontario, who was committed to reaching out and involving girls who were self-conscious about their coordination or physical skills. In order to motivate more girls off the sidelines and on the playing field, Noreen thought about her girlfriends and the activities they like to share. Organizing a Girls' Night Out event, Noreen threw an after-hours party—an informal social evening of volleyball, music, and pizzas—for the girls she taught.

What amazed Noreen was not only the mingling and

CONFIDENTIALLY YOURS . . .

Rita, an elementary school teacher, was in the middle of a girlfriends' spa night when Hurricane Isabel hit. With everybody stuck at her house all night, she and her girlfriends inducted her four-year-old granddaughter Maria into the art of Girls' Night In. That night, much to her delight, sweet Maria got her nails done and sat in front of a roaring fire with her grandmother's friends, letting the moisturizers and wisdom sink in. If one day Maria thinks she imagined that night, Rita has the photos of her covered in a gooey mask to prove it!

---

socializing that went on, but the playfulness of everyone just mixing it up, relating like girlfriends no matter their age or ability. In fact, it seemed as if the girls innately shared a secret language that they communicated through smiles and physical activity. The girls all viewed Girls' Night Out as an opportunity to get to know other students they didn't normally hang out with, and next time invited their moms to share the evening with them as well. Build it and they will come!

R-E-S-P-E-C-T

In order to teach your daughter the vital significance of the women in her Broad Squad, you have a responsibility to know and respect her lineage—the female members of your family. If your mother and grandmothers were anything like mine, they probably kept their homes together, their husbands in line, and once a week played a mean game of bridge or canasta with their Broad Squad. It's a great gift for your daughter to discover where her "feisty" gene comes from—crazy Aunt Florence?—and to appreciate the respect you feel for your mother or grandmother, who grew up in an era when it was far more intimidating to take her place in the front of the bus.

People are simply drawn to my mother. The friends she has are her friends forever, and then some. That's why I'm so lucky that she's my best friend.

—BRITNEY SPEARS

A Ninety-fifth Birthday—For Women Only!

Joan from St. Louis was turning ninety-five, and wanted a party. She knew how she was going to celebrate this landmark occasion: men out, tequila in. Her eighty-year-old live-in male companion was shuttled to a nearby casino for the weekend, and the celebration began! Daughters, granddaughters, and one great-granddaughter arrived at Joan's home—thirteen in all. They came toting pajamas, air mattresses, sleeping bags, and pillows—everything they needed to set up a pajama party extraordinaire in celebration of Joan's long, happy life. But the party turned into more than that; it was also an opportunity for the younger generations to hear the wise and funny stories of this great pioneer and feminist.

The first order of business was to line up shots of tequila from the bottle of Petrón that Joan received on her ninety-third birthday. Beside it, a large bowl of Jell-O shots infused with liquor augured a weekend of laughter. There was food, drink, and a game the family invented called "How well do you know Joan?" Amid the loud laughter and storytelling, the younger generation saw how the women in their family counted on one another to keep their history alive. For Joan

A DAUGHTER'S WORDS

If there is one thing my mother has taught me, it is the importance of girlfriends. She has always taught me to be strong, willful, and independent. But she also has ingrained in me the philosophy that we cannot go through life alone. I have watched my mom go through career changes and several hairstyles. The one thing that never changes is her core group of girlfriends. Her ability to cherish and keep her girlfriends for as long as she has is something I have always admired. I realize now that her girlfriends are her family. They are the beams that hold her up—the glue that holds together the chipped pieces—or the entire house would fall down. This group of girlfriends not only set an example for each other, but has set an example for their children.

the thrill of having an all-female birthday celebration was hosting four generations of women all together under her roof. And on the floor!

As far as what Joan wanted to pass on to her children about the importance of women in your life, she says it best in her own words: "To live long, I say, you've got to live around young people. It's not bad growing older if you can believe that your daughters, granddaughters, and great-granddaughters are going to be able to hold on to each other for strength, compassion, and laughter. That's what I'm leaving you girls . . . each other. Hold on tight." Oh, Joan, you are one great dame. Happy birthday!!

Bringing It Full Circle

We pass on to our daughters the importance of going through life with a Broad Squad, and eventually they see that as they grow up, their mother and her friends do too. They see that in time, even we gain perspective, and little things about their behavior that used to cause our meltdowns and hysteria don't bother us anymore. As they leave high school, ready to take on the world and their future, they watch us return to our high school reunions, just a little curious about old friends, and ready to make peace with the past. Our accomplishments that used to embarrass them, now make them proud as they claim bragging rights about our lives, and kid us as to what Hollywood starlet should play us in the movie. Our daughters take comfort in the knowledge that while they sail off on their solo adventures, they are in fact reassured, knowing that Mom and her girlfriends will be there for each other in good times and in bad. After all, they've seen us in

> (cont.)
>
> I have been truly blessed to grow up around such strong, independent, opinionated, unique, and truly inspirational women. Each of you inspires me to do better, to love selflessly, to think harder, and to want more from life.
> ALEX THOMOPOULOS (17 years old) on her mother's (CRISTINA FERARRE) girlfriends

the kitchen laughing and cooking, sneaking out the back door for Girls' Night Out, keeping vigil at the hospital when one of us was ill. We have done our job if we have passed on the Secret Language of Girlfriends, and the Girlfriend Rules that will hopefully take them full circle right back to their very own Broad Squad, and all the comfort and joy those lifetime connections will bring.

Top Ten Girlfriend Rules

If we were to pass along to our daughters the top ten girl-friend rules, they would be:

    1. Keep Secrets. It is the first and last rule of Girlfriend Law that we never betray each other's confidences. The best conversations in our secret language usually begin with the whisper of a single phrase: "Now, don't tell a soul . . . but . . ." (Translation: We are now the exclusive members of a charter club founded on one juicy bit of gossip that only we share.) Half the fun of having a Broad Squad is the instant built-in confessional allowing us to share our salacious secrets vis-à-vis men, bosses, and hot flashes, secure in the faith we won't hear our most intimate thoughts repeated over lattes at Starbucks the next morning. Failure to live by this rule cannot be dismissed as information pooling or networking. Mean gossip is a publicly traded commodity cashing in on information for social status. If you are found guilty of breaking the secrecy code, you will be sentenced to a fate of cruel and unusual ostracism by your Broad Squad.

Little girls, just like big girls, need the closeness of friends, as they too share secrets and become emotionally vulnerable by revealing parts of themselves that they would never tell their best friends. In order to protect them from the middle school horror of peer pressure and cliques, you cannot teach this to your daughters early enough. Go into the nursery, peer over her pink crib, and coo, "Now, don't tell a soul, but . . ."

2. Dig Deeper. If you notice your girlfriend has gained noticeable weight and still cannot pass by a Krispy Kreme outlet without buying a six pack, then you know

(regardless of what she says) it stinks right now to be
her. It does no earthly good to comment on her ex-
panding waistline or the hideous shade of fuchsia she
insists on wearing. The truth is your girlfriend has chosen to escape the real world—self-medicating on sugar,
color blindness, and denial. Your job as a member of the
911 emergency girlfriend patrol is to gently probe and
disrobe her, until she allows herself to reveal what she is
really feeling, thereby eliminating the need for the icing
on the cake . . . literally. By teaching our daughters
to treat their friends with respect for their emotional
lives, we may be able to curtail some of that Queen
Bee–Wannabe behavior that shows up like the plague
somewhere around junior high. The reward for digging
deeper? Fast forward to your twenty-fifth high school
reunion when all those snobby girls realize you have
sailed on by, while they peaked in tenth grade.

3. Believe in Each Other. One of the great pleasures
we receive from both our daughters and girlfriends is
the opportunity to play the role of the good mother,
without having to be labeled as the goody-goody. Part

of our secret language is understanding that every girl's dream, like fine lingerie, should be treated with care. For example, we encourage each other to remember our girlhood dreams. So when our ten-year-old daughter comes strutting out of her room dressed in a sequined miniskirt with pillows for boobs announcing she wants to be a rock star, we enthusiastically applaud her lip-synching. (Note to self: Fire off a letter of complaint to Britney Spears's manager.) What we keep alive in each other is the belief that our little girl dreams never die; they just lie in wait until we're ready to put them on our to-do list. There is always some part of us that will yearn to be an astronaut, chef, weather girl, or rock star. If our daughters see us encouraging each other to live out those dreams (no matter our age), they will understand that our lives did not end at forty. Rather, they will understand that re-invention takes a Broad Squad, and that it is never too late to become who you were meant to be.

4. Don't Flaunt It. There is nothing less attractive than a girlfriend lording her life over us like she was the queen of some small country. It's one thing to take credit for your accomplishments, and to be proud of what you've created. It's a whole other toxic bag to manipulate the tales of your own success to twist a girlfriend into feeling badly about herself. We are happy for each other's successes, but we are also just a little freaked out too. The only approved girlfriend behavior is to use your own success as a springboard to encourage your girlfriend that she too can realize her dreams. Flaunting also applies to a new man, new money, and new shoes. Enjoy your life without tormenting others. Passing this lesson on to our daughters is a vital part of our secret language.

5. Ladies First. Simply said, don't put a guy before your girlfriend relationships because he may not be worth it. And stop reading (and I mean cold turkey, pull-the-plug stop reading) those self-help books that instruct you on how to "trap" a man. Are we looking for a genuine satisfying relationship, or are we on safari? We need to encourage each other and teach our daughters it is not necessary to put anyone in a cage to love us. And we should never have to cage ourselves in to find a loving relationship. Being single doesn't mean no one loves you, it simply means you aren't married. That's why it's important to be role models and exhibit behavior that teaches our girls to never stand up a date with a Broad Squad member just because you've received a "better" offer from a guy. Doing so is simply unacceptable.

6. Support Each Other. Back each other up on major decisions. We are all on girl patrol 24/7, which means when she's down, you must step up to the plate. Our daughters grow up watching us help each other through the many cycles of our lives and several big-time changes. It is vital to know that our girlfriends are there for us if we marry, if we divorce, if we change careers, tend to ill parents, return to school, or relocate. If you want to grow up and borrow your friend's evening bag or cashmere shawl, you're going to have to learn to share and support each other, always keeping in mind what's best for HER.

7. Work and Friendship Don't Mix. As a rule, we women want egalitarian relationships. A situation where one girlfriend is the boss and the other is the employee can be an emotional explosion waiting to happen. We don't respond well to girlfriends in positions of power who treat us like we're employees, even if we are. Forming a business with a girlfriend where you enter into an equal partnership, or sharing a flex-hours position is cool. But in circumstances when one close friend has to fetch the morning coffee for the other, it can be Glenn Close in *Fatal Attraction* all over again. Try not to confuse being an employee with being a friend—they are completely different roles with different expectations and rules. To pass on this principle to your daughter, it is important for her to have a mentor other than yourself. That way she can experience the blurred lines of hard work and warm friendship before she gets into hot water.

8. Breaking Up Is Hard To Do. Before you dump a friend, you must reach out and try as hard as you can to repair the damage. The complicated way women learn to connect with each other begins on the playground. Boys tend to hang out in packs, which leads to the anathema they call weekend television sports (with a six-pack). Women form pairs in a very intimate, vulnerable way, so the trauma of "breaking up" with a girlfriend can be almost as painful as ending a romance. In the course of a lifetime we will make and break several friend relationships. Make sure you pass on to your daughter the importance of going to the mat to save a friendship, but also teach her how to let go if need be.

9. Shopping Rules. They don't call it retail therapy for nothing. Shopping is, of course, not only the ultimate stress reliever, it also helps us develop the skills we need to discover outlet malls and bargain sales. From the time our girls are old enough to venture forth into the world alone, one of their first stops is the mall. Three important rules of shopping are to never trust dressing room mirrors, never have three pieces of clothing hanging in the closet with the price tags still on, and never suggest it's time to go (otherwise we could have gone shopping with the guys).

10. Keep the Secret Language Alive! It's simple. Call your gal pal right back. Always remember her birthday. Celebrate her accomplishments. And let her know every day she is a joy in your life . . . that's girlfriend language we all understand. Forever and ever!